THE COLLAPSE OF THE FACT/VALUE DICHOTOMY

AND OTHER ESSAYS

INCLUDING THE ROSENTHAL LECTURES

THE COLLAPSE OF THE
FACT/VALUE DICHOTOMY

AND OTHER ESSAYS

HILARY PUTNAM

HARVARD UNIVERSITY PRESS

CAMBRIDGE, MASSACHUSETTS, AND LONDON, ENGLAND

Second printing, 2003

Library of Congress Cataloging-in-Publication Data
Putnam, Hilary.
   The collapse of the fact/value dichotomy and other essays/Hilary Putnam.
      p. cm.
Includes bibliographical references and index.
ISBN 0-674-00905-3
   1. Values. 2. Facts (Philosophy) 3. Welfare economics. 4. Sen, Amartya Kumar.
I. Title
B945.P873 C65 2002
   121'.8--dc21   2002068617

Designed by Gwen Nefsky Frankfeldt

PREFACE

PART I OF THIS VOLUME consists of the lectures I gave at the invitation of the Rosenthal Foundation and the Northwestern University School of Law in November 2000. These lectures spell out the case against the fact/value dichotomy as that dichotomy has historically been developed and defended and explain the significance of the issue particularly for economics. I know but aware of my own limitations did not try to document, that very similar issues arise in the law.

During the ten years that Amartya Sen was my colleague at Harvard University, I came to appreciate not only his brilliance (which was to earn him the Nobel Prize in economics shortly after he left Harvard for Trinity College, Cambridge) and his idealism, but also the importance of what he calls the "capabilities" approach to welfare economics to perhaps the greatest problem facing humanity in our time, the problem of the immense disparities between richer and poorer parts of the globe. At the heart of that approach is the realization that issues of development economics and issues of ethical theory simply cannot be kept apart. Sen, throughout his career, has drawn on both the resources of mathematical economics and the resources of moral philosophy, including conceptions of human flourishing.

Yet most analytic philosophy of language and much analytic metaphysics and epistemology has been openly hostile to talk of human flourishing, regarding such talk as hopelessly "subjective"— often relegating all of ethics, in fact, to that wastebasket category.

In addition, economics has frequently prided itself on avoiding "metaphysical assumptions" while positively gobbling up logical positivist metaphysics—a state of affairs that has been brilliantly analyzed and criticized by Vivian Walsh in *Rationality, Allocation and Reproduction.*[1] Walsh and I have been close friends for nearly fifty years, and this sorry state of affairs in economics is one that he long ago called to my attention. When the invitation came from Northwestern University School of Law to give the Rosenthal Lectures in November 2000 it seemed to me—and Walsh powerfully encouraged me in this—that this was a perfect opportunity to present a detailed rebuttal of the view that "fact is fact and value is value and never the twain shall meet," a view that implies that the Senian enterprise of bringing economics closer to ethics is logically impossible. This was also an opportunity to present a philosophy of language very different from the logical positivist one that made that Senian enterprise seem so impossible. Of course it is clear that developing a less scientistic account of rationality, an account that enables us to see how reasoning, far from being impossible in normative areas, is in fact indispensable to them, and conversely, understanding how normative judgments are presupposed in all reasoning, is important not only in economics, but—as Aristotle saw—in all of life.

As explained in the Introduction, besides the Rosenthal Lectures, which have been only lightly revised (in particular, although they are now called "chapters" and not "lectures," I hope that the reader will still feel that she is hearing lectures as she reads them), I have collected here also those of my recent essays that directly bear on and help to flesh out the arguments of the Rosenthal Lectures.

As always, this book has been closely read by James Conant and by Ruth Anna Putnam. Their critical questions and helpful suggestions profoundly helped in the revision of the Rosenthal Lectures. Thus this book really has four godparents: Conant, Sen, Walsh, and Ruth Anna.

Cambridge, Massachusetts
Harvard University, 2002

CONTENTS

Introduction   1

I   THE COLLAPSE OF THE FACT/VALUE DICHOTOMY
1   The Empiricist Background   7
2   The Entanglement of Fact and Value   28
3   Fact and Value in the World of Amartya Sen   46

II   RATIONALITY AND VALUE
4   Sen's "Prescriptivist" Beginnings   67
5   On the Rationality of Preferences   79
6   Are Values Made or Discovered?   96
7   Values and Norms   111
8   The Philosophers of Science's Evasion of Values   135
     Notes   147
     Index   183

THE COLLAPSE OF THE
FACT/VALUE DICHOTOMY

AND OTHER ESSAYS

INCLUDING THE ROSENTHAL LECTURES

INTRODUCTION

THE IDEA THAT "VALUE JUDGMENTS ARE SUBJECTIVE" is a piece of philosophy that has gradually come to be accepted by many people as if it were common sense. In the hands of sophisticated thinkers this idea can be and has been developed in different ways. The ones I shall be concerned with hold that "statements of fact" are capable of being "objectively true" and capable, as well, of being "objectively warranted," while value judgments, according to these thinkers, are incapable of object truth and objective warrant. Value judgments, according to the most extreme proponents of a sharp "fact/value" dichotomy, are completely outside the sphere of reason. This book tries to show that from the beginning these views rested on untenable arguments and on over-inflated dichotomies. And these untenable arguments had, as we shall see, important "real world" consequences in the twentieth century.

Although I have criticized the fact/value dichotomy in chapters of previous books, this is the first time I have tried to examine the history of the dichotomy from David Hume to the present day, and to examine its concrete effects particularly in the science of economics.[1] I chose economics because economics is a policy science—economists directly advise governments and non-governmental organizations—and precisely the question this book deals with, the question as to whether "ends," that is to say values, can or cannot be rationally discussed or, to put it differently, whether there is a notion of rationality applicable to normative questions, has been hotly debated in economics for many decades. Another reason is that, although at one time the ruling view in economics was precisely the view this book attacks, the view that, as Lionel Robbins put it, "there is no room for argument" when values are in question, a powerful case on the other side, a case for the need for and possibility of reasoned arguments about ethical questions in welfare economics, has been made and defended for many years by one of the world's great economists, Amartya Sen.[2] In our time, then, the question as to what the differences are between "factual" judgments and "value" judgments is no ivory-tower issue. Matters of—literally—life and death may well be at stake.

The first three chapters of this volume, which consist of the Rosenthal Lectures I gave at Northwestern University School of Law in 2000, spell out the case against the fact/value dichotomy as it has historically been developed and defended and explain the significance for economics. In the first of these lectures (Chapter 1), however, I discuss the phenomenon of the elevation of what look like harmless distinctions into absolute dichotomies by philosophers in a more general setting. In particular, I show how the idea of an absolute dichotomy between "facts" and "values" was from the beginning dependant upon a second dichotomy, one unfamiliar to most non-philosophers, the dichotomy of "analytic" and "synthetic" judgments. "Analytic" is a term introduced by Kant for what most people call "definitional" truths, for example, "All bachelors are unmarried." The logical positivist claimed that mathematics consists of analytic truths. "Synthetic" was Kant's term for the *non*-analytic truths, and he took it for granted that synthetic truths state "facts." His surprising claim was that mathematics was both synthetic and a priori. This book tries to show that these two dichotomies, "fact versus value judgment" and "fact versus analytic truth," have corrupted our thinking about both ethical reasoning and description of the world, not least of all by preventing us from seeing how evaluation and description are interwoven and interdependent.

Part II begins with a chapter which is a natural afterword to the Rosenthal lectures, describing, as it does, Sen's earliest wrestling with the fact/value issue. The remainder of Part II (and the book) collects a number of my recent essays and lectures that supplement the arguments of Part I in different directions. Chapter 5 contains a criticism of one of the assumptions ("completeness") of the "rational choice theory" on which much of twentieth-century economics was based. As the reader who looks at the notes will see, the completeness assumption is one that has also come under fire from Amartya Sen (and a number of other economists and philosophers as well). In the second part of Chapter 5, however, I move from pure economics and try to show that the widely discussed distinction between "internal reasons" and "external reasons" for a choice introduced by Bernard Williams is another example of what I call a metaphysical "dichotomy" in Chapter 1, and that it too, albeit more subtly, founders on the entanglement of fact and value that I discuss in Chapter 2.

In Chapters 6 and 7, I discuss two questions dealing with the foundations of ethics. Chapter 6 considers the question of how a belief in the objectivity of ethical judgment is to be defended if one refuses (as I do) to postulate any special "Platonic" realm of "ethical properties." I argue that a basis for a thoroughly non-Platonic account can be found in the writings of John Dewey. In Chapter 7, I consider the position of Jürgen Habermas, who draws a sharp distinction between universal ethical "norms" and non-universalizable values, and who argues that only the former—the "norms"—are objective. Since the goods that economists and philosophers who follow Sen think we must attempt, however tentatively and fallibilistically, to rank-order (for example, longevity, health, access to education at a variety of levels, the opportunity to create and enjoy works of art, and so on) are "values" and not "norms," this would again imply that Sen is asking us to perform the impossible task of reasoning about what is merely subjective, or at least wholly culture-relative. I argue, once again, that we have here an indefensible dichotomy, and that, in fact, the objectivity Habermas posits for norms *presupposes* the objectivity of at least some values.

Beginning in Chapter 2, I argue (following Peirce and the other classical pragmatists) that science itself presupposes values—that *epistemic* values (coherence, simplicity, and the like) are values, too, and in the same boat as ethical values with respect to objectivity. Chapter 8, my concluding chapter, fleshes out this argument by looking at twentieth-century philosophy of science and its sorry history of trying to evade this issue.

I THE COLLAPSE OF THE FACT/VALUE DICHOTOMY

1 | THE EMPIRICIST BACKGROUND

Where is that matter of fact that we call *crime;* point it out; determine the time of its existence; describe its essence or nature; explain the sense or faculty to which it discovers itself. It resides in the mind of the person who is ungrateful. He must, therefore, feel it and be conscious of it. But nothing is there except the passion of ill will or of absolute indifference. You cannot say that these, of themselves, always, and in all circumstances, are crimes. No, they are only crimes when directed towards persons who have before expressed and displayed good-will towards us. Consequently, we may infer, that the crime of ingratitude is not any particular *fact;* but arises from a complication of circumstances which being presented to the spectator excites the *sentiment* of blame, by the particular structure and fabric of his mind.

—DAVID HUME

EVERY ONE of you has heard someone ask, "Is that supposed to be a fact or a value judgment?" The presupposition of this "stumper" is that if it's a "value judgment" it can't possibly be a [statement of] "fact"; and a further presupposition of this is that value judgments are "subjective." The view that value judgments are not factual claims and the inference that if they are not then they must be subjective have a long history. In this century many social scientists accepted both, with terribly important consequences, as we shall see in detail (in connection with the case of economics in particular) in Chapter 3.

Before we explore the dichotomy between facts and values in more detail, it will be helpful to look at a different distinction, one that has also been inflated into a dichotomy and wielded as if it comprised an exhaustive classification of all possible judgments, namely the distinction between analytic and synthetic. "Analytic" is a philosopher's term of art that, under the pressure of developments in the history of early analytic philosophy, came to be viewed as a name for the class of truths that are "tautologies," or "true simply in virtue of their meaning." A favorite example of such an allegedly analytic truth is "All bachelors are unmarried." (The positivists, in employing the terms "analytic" and "synthetic," were borrowing vocabulary from Kant—vocabulary that had passed through and, on the way, been transformed by Frege.)[1] The logical positivists claimed that mathematics consists of analytic truths. "Synthetic" was Kant's term for the *non*-analytic truths. His surprising claim was that mathematical truths are both synthetic and necessary (a priori). In the twentieth century, Kant's positivist opponents attempted to expand the notion of the "analytic" to embrace all of mathematics (which they claimed to be, in effect, a matter of our linguistic *conventions* as opposed to *facts*). Thus for the positivists both distinctions, the distinction between facts and values and the distinction between analytic and synthetic, contrast "facts" with something else: the first contrasts "facts" with "values" and the second contrasts "facts" with "tautologies" (or "analytic truths").

It is widely recognized since Quine's 1951 attack on this overblown form of the analytic-synthetic dichotomy that it has collapsed. (In effect, Quine argued that scientific statements cannot be neatly separated into "conventions" and "facts.") In Chapter 2, I shall describe the phenomenon (or more accurately the "phenomena") that I have called "the entanglement of fact and value" and explain why the existence of such an entanglement undermines the whole idea of an omnipresent and all-important gulf between value judgments and so-called statements of fact.[2] I shall draw upon this phenomenon to argue that this dichotomy collapses in a way that is entirely analogous with the collapse of the analytic-synthetic dichotomy. (Indeed, that distinction, too, collapsed because of a kind of entanglement—the entanglement of convention and fact.)[3] In Chapter 3 (which was the final lecture, when these three chapters were given as Rosenthal Lectures), I shall examine the work of a great economist-philosopher, Amartya Sen, with the aim of seeing how the very nature of "classical theory" in economics becomes transformed in his work and how that transformation is a direct function of the collapse of the fact/value dichotomy.

A version of each of these dichotomies, the fact/value dichotomy ("is" versus "ought") and the analytic-synthetic dichotomy ("matters of fact" versus "relations of ideas"), was foundational for classical empiricism as well as for its twentieth-century daughter, logical positivism. Thus to come to think without these dogmas is to enter upon a *genuine* "post-modernism"—to enter a whole new field of intellectual possibilities in every important area of culture.

I shall begin with some general remarks about dichotomies and distinctions and then address the analytic-synthetic and fact/value dichotomies in particular.

A DISTINCTION IS NOT A DICHOTOMY: THE ANALYTIC AND THE SYNTHETIC

The point of view concerning the relation between "facts" and "values" that I shall be defending in this book is one that John Dewey defended throughout virtually all of his long and exemplary career. Dewey's target was not the idea that, for certain purposes, it might help to draw a distinction (say, between "facts" and "values"); rather his target was what he called the fact/value "dualism." It is one of a great many such philosophical dualisms that Dewey was concerned to identify, diagnose, and exorcise from our thinking. A misunderstanding that his work always tends to provoke (as I have learned by teaching it) is the misunderstanding that when Dewey attacks what he called "dualisms" he is thereby attacking all allied philosophical *distinctions*. Nothing could be further from the truth. Although it was not one of Dewey's favorite examples of a pernicious philosophical dualism, the case of the analytic-synthetic dichotomy illustrates the importance of respecting the distinction between a philosophical dualism and a philosophical distinction.

The logical positivists famously introduced a tripartite classification of all our putative judgments into those that are "synthetic" (and hence, according to the logical positivists, empirically verifiable or falsifiable), those that are "analytic" (and hence, according to the logical positivists, "true [or false] on the basis of the [logical] rules alone"), and those—and this, notoriously, included all our ethical, metaphysical, and aesthetic judgments—that are "cognitively meaningless" (although they may have a practical function as disguised imperatives, ways of influencing one another's attitudes, and so on).[4] Although our ordinary language is confused and vague so that an ordinary-language sentence may not be clearly classifiable as analytic or synthetic (or even as cognitively meaningful or meaningless), once what the speaker is trying to say is made clear, perhaps by offering the speaker a set of precise alternative formulations in an artificially constructed language, whichever *clear* formulation (or "rational reconstruction") she may choose of what she is trying to say will be (1) true (or false) in virtue of the very rules (or conventions) of the artificially constructed language; or (2) testable by confrontation with "observation sentences"; or (3) "cognitively speaking," just *nonsense*. What I said earlier about the fact/value dichotomy, namely that it was conceived as an "omnipresent and all-important gulf," could also be said about the manner in which the positivists conceived the analytic-synthetic dichotomy. To say that it was "omnipresent" is to say that this distinction was conceived of as something that could be applied to absolutely *every* meaningful judgment in absolutely every area. Indeed, if a judgment could not be so classified, then that would suffice to show that, at best, the supposed "judgment" was ambiguous, that the speaker was confused as to which of several different judgments she wanted to make, and that, at worst, there was no real judgment there at all. Such an "analytic-synthetic distinction" (or, to use Dewey's term, such a "dualism" of the analytic and the synthetic) is a metaphysical bogey. To say that the analytic-synthetic distinction appeared "all important" is to say that if one accepted that distinction (or rather dualism), then all philosophical problems would thereby appear to be solved at once! The only problems that would remain are technical problems—such as the ones the logical positivists set themselves.

The crucial transition—to which Dewey sought to alert us—from an innocent distinction to a metaphysical dualism can already be seen in Kant's way of conceiving the distinction between analytic and synthetic judgments. For Kant forced the question: "Are the truths of mathematics analytic or synthetic?" (as well as a similar question about many other hard cases, for example, the principle of causality). Kant found that the principles of mathematics are both synthetic *and* a priori, but that claim has proven anathema to empiricists. The logical positivists' reply was that the principles of mathematics are indeed necessary (as Kant thought), but not synthetic—they are analytic.[5] But in order to give this reply, the logical positivists stretched the notion of analyticity to the breaking point.

Once Kant's category of the synthetic a priori ceases to be available, it becomes important to consider—as many metaphysicians are still unwilling to consider—the possibility that the principles of mathematics are *unlike* both paradigm examples of analytic truths (like "all bachelors are unmarried") *and* purely descriptive truths (like "robins have feathers"). This illustrates one difference between an ordinary distinction and a metaphysical dichotomy: ordinary distinctions have ranges of application, and we are not surprised if they do not always apply.

Not only did the logical positivists follow Kant in supposing that the forced question "analytic or synthetic" must make sense as applied to mathematics, but they thought it must make sense as applied to every single statement of theoretical physics. Thus—notwithstanding the fact that considerations of elegance (which would be classified by the logical positivists as introducing an element of "convention"), as well as the need to make our physical theories as a whole square with experiment ("fact," in the logical positivist idiom), shape the way we develop and employ concepts in physics—they had to maintain that to ask whether, say, the Principle of the Conservation of Energy is "analytic or synthetic" is not only to ask a meaningful question, but to ask one that must be answered if we are to embark upon the project of making our physics (fully) "rational." Quine criticized the positivists, first, for their "failure to appreciate that this legislative trait [in other words, the element of convention] is a trait of scientific hypothesis very generally" (rather than a trait possessed by certain particular scientific sentences and not others), and second, for their "failure to appreciate that it is a trait of the passing event rather than of the truth which is thereby instituted" (in other words, the fact that a sentence is initially adopted as a convention does not mean that it does not subsequently face the tribunal of experiment on a par with all the other sentences of the theory).[6] Summing all this up in a brilliant metaphor, Quine wrote, "The lore of our fathers is a fabric of sentences. In our hands it develops and changes, through more or less arbitrary and deliberate revisions and additions of our own, more or less directly occasioned by the continuing stimulation of our sense organs. It is a pale grey lore, black with fact and white with convention. But I have found no substantial reasons for concluding that there are any quite black threads in it, or any white ones."[7]

Quine, however, went much too far in his initial attack on the distinction in his famous essay "Two Dogmas of Empiricism," throwing out the baby with the bathwater by, in effect, denying that there is *any* sense to distinguishing a class of analytic truths (for example, "all bachelors are unmarried") from truths that are subject to observational test ("all main sequence stars are red").[8] And indeed, much of Quine's philosophy of mathematics seems to be an attempt to assimilate mathematical truth to truth in physics (which would seem to imply that mathematical sentences are "synthetic" in Kant's sense, rather than implying that the question "analytic or synthetic" is a hopelessly unclear one). Others, however, starting with myself, have argued that one can accept Quine's insight (that there are large ranges of statements that cannot be simply classified as either analytic truths or statements of observable fact) while retaining the modest idea that there are also cases that fall on either side of the following specifiable distinction: statements of a language that are trivially true in virtue of the meanings of their words and statements that are not;[9] Quine himself later conceded that I was right and attempted to state that difference precisely.[10] I would add that recognizing a difference between such trivially true statements, however we characterize that class linguistically, and other sorts of statements, does not entail that all those other sorts of statements fall into a single class of "statements about matters of fact" (Hume) or a single class of "synthetic statements" (Kant). In short, it turns out that the notion of an analytic statement can be a modest and occasionally useful notion, but so domesticated that it ceases to be a powerful philosophical weapon that can perform such marvelous functions as explaining why mathematical truths pose no problem at all for empiricism.[11]

Another point about the analytic-synthetic dichotomy, one I have already made in passing but one that perhaps deserves to be repeated, is that as long as the dichotomy was thought to be philosophically obligatory, *both* sides of the distinction were thought to be natural kinds, each a category whose members possessed an "essential" property in common. This meant, for the positivists, not only that all the members of the (thus inflated) category of the analytic were supposed to have the property of being "true [merely] on the basis of the rules of the language," but also that the members of the complementary class, the *non-analytic* statements, were all supposed to have *the* property of being "descriptions of fact," where the original model of a fact is the sort of empirical fact one can *picture*.[12] The possibility that there are many *kinds* of statements that are "not analytic," and the possibility that to identify a statement as not being "analytic" was not (yet) to identify a philosophically interesting *kind* of statement, were missing from the beginning.

THE HISTORY OF THE FACT/VALUE DICHOTOMY

The history of the fact/value dichotomy parallels in certain respects the history of the analytic-synthetic dichotomy. Like the latter, it is foreshadowed by a Humean dichotomy—the one implicit in Hume's famous doctrine that one cannot infer an "ought" from an "is."[13]

Although Hume's claim that one cannot infer an "ought" from an "is" is widely accepted (sometimes this is called "Hume's Law"), the reasons that Hume gave in support of it are by no means accepted by those who cite Hume so approvingly.[14]

One clue that the claim presupposes a substantial metaphysics (as opposed to being a simple logical point) is that no one, including Hume himself, ever takes it as merely a claim about the validity of certain forms of inference, analogous to the claim "you cannot infer 'p&q' from 'p or q.'" Indeed, if the claim were simply one about the *form* of certain inferences, it would prohibit one from ever inferring "you ought to do x in such-and-such circumstances" from "for you to do x in such-and-such circumstances is good, and for you to refrain from doing x in those circumstances is bad." Of course, many philosophers would reply to this example by saying that it does not run afoul of Hume's dictum because it is a case of inferring an "ought" from an "ought." But that is my point. Their ability to recognize statements such as "for you to do x in such-and-such circumstances is good, and for you to refrain from doing x in those circumstances is bad" as a case of an "ought" turns not on any feature of the form of the statement but rather on an understanding of its content.

Nor did Hume himself (or any of his readers) understand the claim as one about the canons of formal inference. Rather, Hume assumed a metaphysical dichotomy between "matters of fact" and "relations of ideas" (the dichotomy that constituted his early anticipation of "the analytic-synthetic distinction"). What Hume meant was that when an "is" judgment describes a "matter of fact," then no "ought" judgment can be derived from it. Hume's metaphysics of "matters of fact" constitutes the whole ground of the alleged underivability of "oughts" from "ises."

However, Hume's criterion for "matters of fact" presupposed what might be called a "pictorial semantics."[15] Concepts, in Hume's theory of the mind, are a kind of "idea," and "ideas" are themselves pictorial: the only way they can represent any "matter of fact" is by *resembling* it (not necessarily visually, however—ideas can also be tactile, olfactory, and so on). Ideas have, however, nonpictorial properties as well; they can involve or be associated with *sentiments*, in other words, emotions. Hume does not just tell us that one cannot infer an "ought" from an "is"; he claims, more broadly, that there is no "matter of fact" about *right* and no matter of fact about *virtue*.[16] The reason is that if there *were* matters of fact about virtue and vice, then it would have to be the case (if we assume "pictorial semantics") that the property of virtue would be *picturable* in the way that the property of being an apple is picturable. Hume was quite correct, *given his semantical views*, to conclude that there are no such matters of fact. Furthermore, *given that "passions" or "sentiments" were the only remaining properties of "ideas," Hume thought he had at his disposal to explain why it so much as seems to us that there are such matters of fact*, it was quite reasonable for him to conclude that the components of our "ideas" that correspond to judgments of virtue and vice are nothing more than "sentiments" aroused in us by the "contemplation" of the relevant actions owing to "the particular structure and fabric" of our minds.[17]

The doctrine that "one cannot infer an 'ought' from an 'is'" possesses a feature that I noted in connection with the analytic-synthetic dichotomy: one side of the distinction names a class with a more or less distinctive feature. In the case of Hume's moral philosophy, the class is the class of judgments that involve the "idea" *ought*. So described, the class presupposes the discredited seventeenth- and eighteenth-century talk of "ideas," but (if we wish to *disinflate* the dichotomy implicit in Hume's arguments) we can repair this defect by speaking instead of the class of judgments that involve the word "ought" in one of its ethical uses. To be sure, so described, the class is somewhat vague (since it is not clear when a use of "ought" is an "ethical" use), but just as in the case of the notion of an "analytic truth," it would be premature to deny that there is such a class at all merely on the grounds of the vagueness of its boundaries. Moreover, guided by Hume's own remarks in his *Enquiry Concerning the Principles of Morals*, we can enlarge the class by considering judgments containing not only the word "ought," but also "right," "wrong," "virtue," "vice," and such derivatives as "virtuous" and "vicious," as well as "good" and "bad" in their ethical uses.[18] The resulting class—call it the class of *paradigmatic value judgments*—would contain the great majority of examples that appear in the writings of the proponents of what I am calling the fact/value "dichotomy." Conceding that there is indeed a class (albeit with somewhat vague boundaries) of truths that may be called "analytic" in and of itself neither (1) appears to solve any philosophical problems, nor (2) tells us precisely *what* the members of the class have in common, nor (3) requires us to concede that the complement of the class (the class of the non-analytic truths and falsehoods) is a natural kind whose members possess some sort of common essence. Similarly, conceding that there is a class of (paradigmatically ethical) judgments that contain perhaps nine or ten or a dozen familiar ethical words neither solves any philosophical problems, nor tells us what exactly makes a word an *ethical* word, nor requires us to concede that all the non-ethical judgments fall into one or even two or three natural kinds.

The role of Kant in the further evolution of what was to become the contemporary fact/value dichotomy is too complex to go into here in any detail because his philosophy itself is too complex to admit of a brief discussion. Suffice it to say that many Kantian moral philosophers have *taken* Kant to say—and have agreed with Kant, so interpreted—that value judgments have the character of *imperatives* (Kant himself speaks of "rules" and "maxims" as well as of the famous "Categorical Imperative"). According to them, "murder is wrong" is a way of saying "do not murder," and this is not a description of any fact (this then becomes a point on which Kant—so interpreted—agrees with Hume). But, on any sound interpretation of Kant's view, such a remark cannot be just an expression of a "sentiment" either; nor can it be simply a mixture of a judgment (that certain circumstances obtain) together with an expression of a "sentiment" (with respect to those circumstances). Here Kant strongly disagrees with Hume. All interpreters of Kant take him to hold that moral statements can be *rationally justified*—indeed, the whole of Kant's moral philosophy is an account of how this can be the case.

While there are some distinguished moral philosophers (for example, Barbara Herman and Christine Korsgaard) who think Kant's account—at least as reconstructed by John Rawls—is fundamentally right, most philosophers today find Kant's moral philosophy overly dependent on the rest of Kant's metaphysics, which few if any philosophers are able any longer to accept.[19] And, just as the collapse of the philosophical credibility of Kant's notion of a "synthetic a priori truth" led the logical positivists to go back to a vastly inflated version of Hume's idea that a judgment is either analytic (deals with "relations of ideas") or synthetic a posteriori (deals with "matters of fact"), and also led them to expand the analytic (since the classic empiricist attempt to show that mathematics is synthetic a posteriori didn't work), so the collapse of the philosophical credibility of Kant's notion of "pure practical reason" (and with it of the Kantian variety of a priori ethics founded on that notion) led the logical positivists to go back to a vastly inflated version of Hume's idea that ethical judgments are not statements of fact but either expressions of sentiment or disguised imperatives.[20] In this latter idea a residual Kantian influence is still evident but with a Humean twist: for the positivist, these imperatives *cannot* be rationally justified, but simply reflect, at bottom, the "volitional" state of the speaker.

This exclusion of ethical statements from the domain of rational discourse is given vehement expression by Carnap in his little book *The Unity of Science*.[21] After explaining that all nonscientific problems are "a confusion of . . . pseudoproblems," he writes:

> All statements belonging to Metaphysics, regulative Ethics, and (metaphysical) Epistemology have this defect, are in fact unverifiable and, therefore, unscientific. In the Viennese Circle, we are accustomed to describe such statements as nonsense (after *Wittgenstein*).[22] This terminology is to be understood as implying a logical, not say a psychological distinction; its use is intended to assert only that the statements in question do not possess a certain logical characteristic common to all proper scientific statements [namely, verifiability—HP]; we do not intend to assert the impossibility of associating any conceptions or images with these logically invalid statements. Conceptions can be associated with any arbitrarily compounded series of words; and metaphysical statements are richly evocative of associations and feelings both in authors and readers.[23]

In both the cases of the analytic-synthetic distinction and the fact/value distinction, one can observe that one side of each of these distinctions (which become inflated into metaphysical dichotomies) names a class with a more or less distinctive feature. The paradigms for the class of truths that formed the analytic side of Kant's analytic-synthetic distinction were truths of the form "all As are Bs," where the subject A "contains" the property denoted by the predicate term B, for example, "all bachelors are unmarried," and logical consequences of these, for example, "there are no married bachelors," and so on.[24]

The fact/value distinction/dichotomy came into being somewhat differently in that Hume did not introduce any single term for what we now call "value judgments" (though he did have the term "morals"). Instead, he discusses individual value terms, for example, "crime," "ought," "virtue," and the like. But the context is always the context of *ethics*. Thus the class of value terms under discussion is, almost invariably, the class of terms that figure centrally in examples of ethical judgments in the writings of philosophers.

Ever since Hume, the fact that there are many kinds of value judgment that are not themselves of an ethical (or "moral") variety tends to get sidelined in philosophical discussions of the relation between (so-called) values and (so-called) facts. This is especially true of the positivists. Carnap generally speaks not of "value judgments" but only of the statements of "regulative ethics" (or sometimes "normative ethics"). Reichenbach, when he turns to the "value" side of the fact/value dichotomy, writes of "The Nature of Ethics."[25] And in Charles Stevenson's book *Facts and Values* there is not a single reference to any value judgments outside of ethics! It is not that these authors would deny that, say, aesthetic judgments are cases of value judgments, but, for the most part, their real target is the supposed objectivity or rationality of ethics, and in disposing of this topic, they take themselves to have provided an account that covers all other kinds of value judgment as well.[26]

If we *disinflate* the fact/value dichotomy, what we get is this: there is a distinction to be drawn (one that is useful in some contexts) between ethical judgments and other sorts of judgments. This is undoubtedly the case, just as it is undoubtedly the case that there is a distinction to be drawn (and one that is useful in some contexts) between *chemical* judgments and judgments that do not belong to the field of chemistry. *But nothing metaphysical follows from the existence of a fact/value distinction in this (modest) sense.*

THE "FACT" SIDE OF THE DICHOTOMY

One way to summarize the preceding conclusion is as follows: the fact/value dichotomy is, at bottom, not a *distinction* but a *thesis*, namely the thesis that "ethics" is not about "matters of fact." In Hume's case, the thesis was not meant to rule out the possibility of a philosopher's writing a textbook on morals, whereas in Carnap's case it certainly was so meant. (In the quotation from *The Unity of Science* above, ethical utterances were allowed no more meaning than "any arbitrarily compounded series of words"!) Hume was able to combine his noncognitivism in ethics with a faith in the existence of such a thing as ethical *wisdom* because he shared the comfortable eighteenth-century assumption that all intelligent and well-informed people who mastered the art of thinking about human actions and problems impartially would feel the appropriate "sentiments" of approval and disapproval in the same circumstances unless there was something wrong with their personal constitution. This has led a number of commentators to misread Hume as claiming that what "good" *means* is "such as to cause most impartial and well informed people to approve"; but this is an exegetical mistake. Hume thinks that most impartial and well-informed people *will* approve of whatever is good, but he *never* claims that this is the content of the "idea" of good; if he did, he would not claim that there is no "fact" that is the fact that something is a virtue or a vice, and so on, and he does quite clearly make that claim. Concerning, for example, the concept of *crime*, in the eighteenth-century sense of "a grievous moral wrong" (not the modern merely legal sense), Hume writes: "the crime of ingratitude is not any particular *fact;* but arises from a complication of circumstances which being presented to the spectator excites the *sentiment* of blame, by the particular structure and fabric of his mind" (emphasis in the original). However, Hume's interest in the (noncognitive) character of ethical concepts was part of a wider interest in *ethics as such.*[27] His analysis of the nature of ethical judgments was preliminary to the general treatment of an entire self-standing branch of philosophy—morals—the proper reconstruction of which he took to have broad social and political implications. By the time we get to someone like C. L. Stevenson this wider interest has considerably faded, and in Carnap and many of his followers such an interest is pointedly absent.[28] Carnap's purpose was to *expel* ethics from the domain of knowledge, not to *reconstruct* it. But the confidence of the logical positivists that they could expel ethics from the domain of the rationally discussable was in part derived from the way in which the analytic-synthetic and fact/value dualisms reinforced one another in their hands. According to the positivists, in order to be knowledge, ethical "sentences" would have to be either analytic, which they manifestly are not, or else "factual." And their confidence that they could not be factual, just like Hume's confidence that "the crime of ingratitude is not any particular fact," derived from their confidence that they knew exactly what a *fact* was. In the writings of the positivists, in the cases of both the dualism of analytic and factual statements and the dualism of ethical and factual judgments, it is the conception of the "factual" that does all the philosophical work.

But science had changed radically since Hume's day, and the positivists found themselves pressed more and more to abandon their initial notion of a fact, which was somewhat similar to Hume's, in order to do justice to the revolutionary science of the first half of the twentieth century. And in revising their notion of a fact, I shall argue, they destroyed the very basis on which they erected the fact/value dichotomy!

In Hume's day, it was not unreasonable to maintain that there were no scientifically indispensable predicates that refer to entities not observable with the human senses.[29] "Atoms" did, to be sure, figure in a great deal of (primarily British) scientific *speculation* at the time, but Locke had held that we could never *know* anything about them, and Berkeley and Hume were quite willing to dismiss such speculations as unintelligible, just as they were willing to regard talk of points in geometry or infinitesimals in calculus as (philosophically speaking) unintelligible.[30]

Indeed, the Humean notion of a "fact" is simply something of which there can be a sensible "impression." When Hume asks, for example, what is the factual component in the notion of *causation* and what added to the fact by a sort of projection, and decides that it is the idea of necessitation (in other words, of *bringing about*) that is added by projection, all Hume has to do is to ask whether there is such a thing as an "impression" of necessitation. (It is indeed interesting that so many philosophers who continue to think that Hume "showed" that there is no such thing as an ethical fact today reject the identical arguments that Hume offered in connection with *causation!*)

At the time that the Vienna circle was formed, however, the situation was very different. Bacteria, which are not "observables" in the logical positivist sense, were known to exist (observed with the aid of the microscope), and although the reality of "atoms" was denied by some of the world's best physicists prior to Perrin's experiments on Brownian motion in 1909, after those experiments working physicists (though not such physicist-philosophers as Mach and Bridgman) were almost all prepared to regard them as perfectly real things. Moreover, the internal structure of atoms was rapidly being discovered—electrons, protons, neutrons, followed by positrons, mesons, and a host of other particles became a large part of the physicist's everyday ontology. The logical positivists themselves were deeply impressed by the successes of relativity theory, which speaks of "curved space-time," and quantum mechanics. The idea that a "fact" is just a sensible "impression" would hardly seem to be tenable any longer.

Yet the logical positivists held out against conceding this for more than a decade.[31] Carnap's celebrated *Der logische Aufbau der Welt* (The Logical Construction of the World), published in 1928, held that all factual statements are transformable into statements about the subjects' own sense experiences or *Elementarerlebnisse*. Indeed, some members of the Vienna circle even insisted that a meaningful statement must be *conclusively verifiable* by confrontation with direct experience![32] At bottom, the original logical positivist view was that a "fact" was something that could be certified by mere observation or even a mere report of a sensory experience. If *this* is the notion of a fact, then it is hardly surprising that ethical judgments turn out not to be "factual"!

Carnap, however, held out against the requirement of *conclusive* verifiability; and, in 1936, he slightly liberalized the requirement that all factual predicates must be definable by means of observation terms. But it still remained the case that (1) a necessary condition that a statement had to meet to be counted as "cognitively meaningful" was that it be expressible in "the language of science" (as formalized by the logical positivists) and (2) the predicates admitted into the "factual" part of the language of science had to be "observation terms" or reducible (by specified and limited means) to observation terms.[33] (Other, mathematical and logical, predicates could be admitted into the "analytic" part.) The dismaying consequence was that statements about bacteria or electrons or *the* gravitational field would either have to be counted as "nonsense" (along with "metaphysics" and "normative ethics") or else have to be "reduced" to observation terms. Either we never *really* talk about atoms at all (such talk is just a *façon de parler*, just as so many physicists had thought before the Perrin experiments), or if we do, and if such talk is indeed "cognitively meaningful," then the logical positivists' "criterion of significance" would have to be radically revised. By 1938, Carnap had come to the conclusion that the latter was the only possible course to take.

The revision involved totally jettisoning the requirement that a meaningful factual predicate must be either an observation predicate or "reducible" to observation predicates. In his 1938 "Foundations of Logic and Mathematics,"[34] Carnap conceded that (as the British physicist-philosopher Norman Campbell had long insisted)[35] such troublesome terms as "electron" and "charge" do not enter physics through definitions (or even "reductions") but are simply "taken as primitive."[36] As long as the system as a whole enables us to predict our experiences more successfully than we could without them, such "abstract terms" are to be accepted as "empirically meaningful." But this turned out to raise a host of problems![37]

One obvious problem has to do with the question that is our concern at the moment: what *exactly* did the logical positivists, who were the most influential marketers of the fact/value dichotomy, understand by *fact*? On the revised logical positivist criterion of cognitive significance, it is the *system of scientific statements as a whole* that has "factual content." But what about the individual statements?

Here Carnap's view remained strongly influenced by classical empiricism.[38] In his subsequent writings, Carnap continued to distinguish sharply between the "observation terms," in other words, the vocabulary that refers to "observable properties," which he now said are "completely interpreted,"[39] in other words, which have freestanding meaning, and the "theoretical terms," such as "bacterium," "electron," and "gravitational field," which he said are "only partially interpreted." In effect, although such terms were admitted to the language of science, they were regarded as mere devices for deriving the sentences that *really* state the empirical facts, namely the observation sentences.

THE POVERTY OF THE LOGICAL POSITIVIST CONCEPTION OF A LANGUAGE

As we saw earlier, Carnap simply dismissed normative ethics as "nonsense" without any detailed examination of a single ethical concept. However, I have heard it suggested that Carnap would have cheerfully admitted the existence of (and even the importance of) concepts that defy simple classification as "descriptive or normative"—concepts like the concept of cruelty, which we shall discuss in detail in the next chapter—*in ordinary language.*[40] The suggestion is that "all" he would have insisted on was that when we *rationally reconstruct* our language we need to make a "sharp and clear" distinction between value terms and descriptive terms.

Well, let us imagine that a historian describes some Roman emperor as "cruel," and Carnap asks, "do you intend that as a value judgment or as a description?" We suppose that the historian says, "As a description." What would Carnap say next?

It is quite clear what he would say. He would first ask, "If cruel is being used as a descriptive predicate in your history, is it an *observa-*

tion term or a *theoretical term?* (The observational-theoretical dichotomy itself came under sharp attack, starting in 1960, but
that dichotomy was absolutely essential to Carnap's own later project of the "rational reconstruction" of domains of meaningful discourse.)[41]

Carnap also required that the list of "observation terms" contain
only terms referring to properties "for which the test procedure is
extremely simple (as in the . . . examples just mentioned)." The examples just mentioned (in his last lengthy paper on this subject)
were *blue, hot, large, warmer than,* and *contiguous with.*[42] Obviously
cruelty is not a property "for which the test procedure is extremely
simple (as in the . . . examples just mentioned)." (It is also not an
"observable disposition" in Carnap's technical sense.)[43] This leaves
only the possibility that it is a "theoretical term." So Carnap will
now ask the historian, "If *cruel* is supposed to be a theoretical term,
what exactly are the *postulates* by which it is introduced?" If the historian now replies that "cruel" is not the name of a hypothetical
physical property like *charge,* which we postulate in order to explain
scientifically and predict certain phenomena, but rather a term that
figures in a certain kind of reflective understanding of the *rationale*
of conduct, in understanding both how the agent feels and acts and
how others perceive the agent's feelings and actions, Carnap would
undoubtedly reply that "you are talking about something that requires Weber's mysterious *Verstehen* or some such process. That is
just metaphysical nonsense."

Carnap thus required cognitively meaningful language to resem-
ble the language of physics. Even though there are very few
philosophers anymore who subscribe to verificationist criteria of
intelligibility of the kind that Carnap proposed, many Anglo-
American analytic philosophers continue to think that meaningful
language must be understood on the model of the language of
physics. (Not all, of course; others, for example, Donald Davidson
and myself, have argued that, for example, ordinary psychological
predicates—even ones which, unlike *cruel,* do not name vices or

virtues—cannot, as a rule, be understood on this model.)[44] The philosophers who subscribe to this way of viewing our language are not logical positivists anymore. But their view of, for example, ordinary-language psychological terms (if they do not dismiss "folk psychology" altogether as being on a par with astrology or alchemy)[45] is that what psychological descriptions *must* refer to are *brain states*—either neurological states[46] or so-called computational (or functional) states, describable in terms of the brain's "software."[47] Carnap himself thought such terms refer to neurological states.[48]

But, on the face of it, the idea that whenever I describe someone as cruel, or as irritated, or as delighted, I am committed to a "theory" according to which there is a "brain-state," either physical or computational in character, such that all cruel (or all irritated, or all delighted) people are in that brain-state, and no one who is not cruel (or irritated, or delighted) is in that brain-state is not a scientific finding at all, but mere science fiction.[49] To force all the descriptive terms that we employ in our everyday discourse into one side or the other of the dichotomy "observation term or theoretical term" is to force them into a Procrustean bed. The logical positivist fact/value dichotomy was defended on the basis of a narrowly scientistic picture of what a "fact" might be, just as the Humean ancestor of that distinction was defended upon the basis of a narrow empiricist psychology of "ideas" and "impressions." The realization that so much of our descriptive language is a living counterexample to *both* (classical empiricist and logical positivist) pictures of the realm of "fact" ought to shake the confidence of anyone who supposes that there is a notion of *fact* that contrasts neatly and absolutely with the notion of "value" supposedly invoked in talk of the nature of all "value judgments."

The example of the predicate "cruel" also suggests that the problem is not just that the empiricist's (and later the logical positivist's) notion of a "fact" was much too narrow from the start. A deeper problem is that, from Hume on, empiricists—and not only empiricists but many others as well, in and outside of philosophy—failed to appreciate the ways in which factual description and valuation can and must be *entangled*. What that means, and what difference the entanglement of fact and value makes, will be the subject of the next chapter.

2 | THE ENTANGLEMENT OF FACT AND VALUE

IN THE PRECEDING CHAPTER I recounted the history of the empiricists' fact/value dichotomy, beginning with "Hume's Law," as it has been called, "No ought from an is."[1]

I began by describing the way in which the notion of a "fact," which underlies Hume's distinction between "matters of fact" and "relations of ideas" (later to become the analytic-synthetic dichotomy) as well as Hume's dictum that an "ought" can never be derived from an "is" (later to become the fact/value dichotomy), was a narrow one in which a fact is something that corresponds to a sense-impression. I then turned to the logical positivists, whose views were enormously influential in persuading the social scientific world at first, and later (perhaps through the influence of sociologists and economists), the learned (and even not-so-learned) world generally of the validity and indispensability of sharply separating "facts" and "values," and I showed that their earliest views of what a fact is were, at bottom, very close to Hume's. I also emphasized that, although Hume himself was an important ethical thinker, the logical positivists did not regard ethics as a possible subject of rational discussion. Indeed, *their* fact/value dichotomy was not based on any serious examination of the nature of values or valuation at all; what they examined—and in a narrow empiricist spirit—was the nature of "fact."

Beginning in 1939, however, the logical positivists liberalized their famous "criterion of cognitive significance," by holding that cognitively meaningful language could contain not only observation terms but also the so-called "theoretical terms," terms referring to unobservables and introduced by systems of postulates, the postulates of the various scientific theories.[2] I summarized the resulting liberalized criterion of cognitive significance by saying that, "as long as the system as a whole enables us to predict our experiences more successfully than we could without them, such predicates [theoretical predicates] are to be accepted as 'empirically meaningful.'" But to *predict* anything means (to logical positivists) to *deduce observation sentences from a theory.* And to deduce anything from a set of empirical postulates, we need not only those postulates but also the axioms of mathematics and logic. According to the logical positivists, these axioms—and many of their consequences, as well as our old friends, the verbal truths like, "All bachelors are unmarried"—do not state "facts" at all. They are *analytic* and thus "empty of factual content." In short, "belonging to the language of science" is (from a logical positivist point of view) a criterion of *scientific* significance, but not everything *scientifically* significant is a statement of *fact;* within the scientifically significant there are, according to the logical positivists, *analytic* as well as *synthetic* (that is, factual) statements. Thus the search for a satisfactory demarcation of the "factual" became the search for a satisfactory way of drawing "the analytic-synthetic distinction."

In 1950, however, Quine demolished the (metaphysically inflated) notion of the "analytic" to the satisfaction of most philosophers.[3]

He did not suggest, however, that every statement in the language of science should be regarded as a statement of "fact" (that is, as "synthetic"); rather, Quine suggested that the whole idea of classifying every statement including the statements of pure mathematics as "factual" or "conventional" (which the logical positivists equated with "analytic") was a hopeless muddle.[4] But if the whole idea that there is a *clear* notion of fact collapsed with the hopelessly restrictive empiricist picture that gave rise to it, *what happens to the fact/value dichotomy?* As the economist-philosopher Vivian Walsh has written, "To borrow and adapt Quine's vivid image, if a theory may be black with fact and white with convention, it might well (as far as logical empiricism could tell) be red with values. Since for them confirmation *or* falsification had to be a property of a theory *as a whole,* they had no way of unraveling this whole cloth."[5]

Thus Walsh (and before him, Quine's friend Morton White)[6] made the point that after Carnap's abandonment (between 1936 and 1939) of the picture of "factual" sentences as individually capable of confrontation with sense experience (which was, as we have seen, just the traditional empiricist picture) and Quine's critique of the logical positivists' picture of what they called the language of science as neatly divided into a "factual" part and an "analytic" part, *the whole argument for the classical fact/value dichotomy was in ruins,* and that, "as far as logical empiricism could tell," science might presuppose values as well as experiences and conventions. Indeed, once we stop thinking of "value" as synonymous with "ethics," it is quite clear that it *does* presuppose values—it presupposes *epistemic* values.

EPISTEMIC VALUES ARE VALUES TOO

The classical pragmatists, Peirce, James, Dewey, and Mead, all held that value and normativity permeate *all* of experience. In the philosophy of science, what this point of view implied is that normative judgments are essential to the practice of science itself. These pragmatist philosophers did not refer only to the kind of normative judgments that we call "moral" or "ethical"; judgments of "coherence," "plausibility," "reasonableness," "simplicity," and of what Dirac famously called the beauty of a hypothesis, are all normative judgments in Charles Peirce's sense, judgments of "what ought to be" in the case of reasoning.[7]

Carnap tried to avoid admitting this by seeking to reduce hypothesis-selection to an *algorithm*—a project to which he devoted most of his energies beginning in the early 1950s, but without success. In Chapter 7, I shall look in detail at this and other unsuccessful attempts by various logical positivists (as well as Karl Popper) to avoid conceding that *theory selection always presupposes values,* and we shall see that they were, one and all, failures. But just as these empiricist philosophers were determined to shut their eyes to the fact that judgments of coherence, simplicity (which is itself a whole bundle of different values, not just one "parameter"), beauty, naturalness, and so on, are presupposed by physical science, likewise many today who refer to values as purely "subjective" and science as purely "objective" continue to shut their eyes to this same fact. Yet *coherence* and *simplicity* and the like are *values.*

THE DIFFERENCE BETWEEN EPISTEMIC AND ETHICAL VALUES (AND WHY ITS SIGNIFICANCE SHOULD NOT BE MISCONSTRUED)

To say that epistemic values are values too, as I have just done, is of course not to deny that there are *differences* between epistemic and ethical values. Indeed, there are differences between the various ethical values themselves; in the Talmud, for example, the difference between God's *din* (justice) and his *hesed* (compassion) is sometimes described as a conflict within God's very being. This image captures something real; justice and compassion are very different concerns, even though both are essential to the ethical life. The concern that is—obviously—connected with the values that guide us in choosing between hypotheses (coherence, simplicity, preservation of past doctrine, and the like) is the concern with "right description of the world," and to many this has seemed to be the same thing as "objectivity." If this were right, then ethical values wouldn't merely be connected with *different* concerns than epistemic values; they would not be connected with objectivity at all. But this is a mistake.

To see the nature of the mistake, it is first of all necessary to be clear on what it does and does not mean to say that epistemic values guide us in pursuing right descriptions of the world. As Roderick Firth pointed out twenty years ago, it is not that we have some way of telling that we have arrived at the truth *apart from* our epistemic values and can, so to speak, run a test to see how often choosing the more coherent, simpler, and so on, theory turns out to be true *without presupposing these very standards of justified empirical belief.*[8] The claim that on the whole we come closer to truth about the world by choosing theories that exhibit simplicity, coherence, past predictive success, and so on, and even the claim that we have made more successful predictions than we would have been able to obtain by relying on Jerry Falwell, or on imams, or on ultra-orthodox rabbis, or simply relying on the authority of tradition, or the authority of some Marxist-Leninist Party, are themselves complex empirical hypotheses that we choose (or which those of us who do choose them choose) because we have been guided by the very values in question in our reflections upon records and testimonies concerning past inquiries—not, of course, all the stories and myths that there are in the world about the past, but the records and testimonies that we have good reason to trust *by these very criteria of "good reason."*

To say this is not to express any sort of skepticism about the superiority of these criteria to criteria provided by (what Peirce called) The Method of Authority and The Method of What is Agreeable to Reason. If this is circular justification, it is still justification enough for most of us. But it is to say that if these epistemic values do enable us to correctly describe the world (or to describe it *more* correctly than any alternative set of epistemic values would lead us to do), that is something we see *through the lenses of those very values*. It does not mean that those values admit an "external" justification.

What of the idea that right description of the world is the same thing as "objectivity"? This idea rests, pretty clearly, on the supposition that "objectivity" means *correspondence to objects* (an idea that corresponds to the etymology of the word, of course). But it is not only normative truths such as "Murder is wrong" that pose counterexamples to this idea; as I argue elsewhere, *mathematical and logic truth* are likewise examples of "objectivity without objects."[9] To be sure, many philosophers tell us that we have to posit peculiar objects (so-called abstract entities) to account for mathematical truth; but this does not help at all, as we can see by asking, "Would mathematics *work* one bit less well if these funny objects *stopped* existing?" Those who posit "abstract entities" to account for the success of mathematics do not claim that we (or any other things in the empirical world) *interact* with the abstract entities. But if any entities do not interact with us or with the empirical world *at all,* then doesn't it follow that *everything would be the same if they didn't exist?* In the case of logical truth, ontological accounts run into well-known difficulties as well, difficulties connected with the central logical notion of "validity."[10]

What I am saying is that it is time we stopped equating *objectivity* with *description*. There are many sorts of statements—bona fide statements, ones amenable to such terms as "correct," "incorrect," "true," "false," "warranted," and "unwarranted"—that are not descriptions, but that are under rational control, governed by standards appropriate to their particular functions and contexts. Enabling us to describe the world is one extremely important function of language; it is not the only function, nor is it the only function to which questions such as, "Is this way of achieving this function reasonable or unreasonable? Rational or irrational? Warranted or unwarranted?" apply.

"THICK" ETHICAL CONCEPTS

The entanglement of facts and values is not limited to the sorts of facts that the logical positivists recognized, and epistemic values. The fact is that although the logical positivists thought that what they called the language of science was the *whole* of "cognitively meaningful" language, their view was profoundly wrong, as I argued in the previous chapter—indeed, it was even self-refuting. It is self-refuting because their key philosophical terms "cognitively meaningful" and "nonsense" are not observation terms, not "theoretical terms" of a physical theory, and not logical/mathematical terms, and these are the only kinds of terms that their language of science was allowed to contain.[11] If we look at the vocabulary of our language as a *whole,* and not the tiny part that was supposed by logical positivism to be sufficient for the description of "facts," we will find a much deeper entanglement of fact and value (including ethical and aesthetic and every other sort of value) even at the level of individual predicates.

The sort of entanglement I have in mind becomes obvious when we study words like "cruel." The word "cruel" obviously—or at least it is obvious to most people, even if it is denied by some famous defenders of the fact/value dichotomy—has normative and, indeed, ethical uses. If one asks me what sort of person my child's teacher is, and I say, "He is very cruel," I have both criticized him as a teacher and criticized him as a man. I do not have to add, "He is not a good teacher," or, "He is not a good man." I might, of course, say, "When he isn't displaying his cruelty, he is a very good teacher," but I cannot simply, without distinguishing the respects in which or the occasions on which he is a good teacher and the respects in which or the occasions on which he is very cruel, say, "He is a very cruel person and a very good teacher." Similarly, I cannot simply say, "He is a very cruel person and a good man," and be understood. Yet "cruel" can also be used purely descriptively, as when a historian writes that a certain monarch was exceptionally cruel, or that the cruelties of the regime provoked a number of rebellions. "Cruel" simply ignores the supposed fact/value dichotomy and cheerfully allows itself to be used sometimes for a normative purpose and sometimes as a descriptive term. (Indeed, the same is true of the term "crime.") In the literature, such concepts are often referred to as "thick ethical concepts."

That the thick ethical concepts are counterexamples to the idea that there exists an absolute fact/value *dichotomy* has long been pointed out, and the defenders of the dichotomy have offered three main responses. (The resulting discussion has resulted in what I think of as some of the best ethical/metaethical discussion of the last century, including outstanding papers and books by Philippa Foot, Iris Murdoch, John McDowell, and David Wiggins criticizing the dichotomy, and rejoinders by R. M. Hare and John Mackie among others.)[12]

One response was contained in Hume's rhetorical question: "Where is that matter of fact that we call *crime?*"—Hume meant "grievous wrong" by *crime*—and his denial that one can point out any such "matter of fact." To accept this response would be to banish all thick ethical concepts to the same limbo of the "emotive" or "noncognitive," that the "thin" (or "thinner") ethical words ("good," "ought," "right," and their opposites "bad," "must-not," "wrong," as well as "virtue," "vice," "duty," "obligation," and so on) were banished to by Hume and his successors. But the number of such words is so great that there has been an obvious reluctance to follow Hume even on the part of the noncognitivists (and their relatives, the so-called "error theorists").[13] Not even David Hume would be willing to classify, for example, "generous," "elegant," "skillful," "strong," "gauche," "weak," or "vulgar" as concepts to which no "fact" corresponds.[14]

The responses that noncognitivists usually make today are rather the following two:

(1)   To simply insist that the thick ethical concepts are plain factual concepts and not ethical or normative concepts at

all. This was the response of R. M. Hare (in the case of "rude") and of John Mackie (in the case of "cruel").

(2) To claim that the thick ethical concepts are "factorable" into a purely descriptive component and an "attitudinal" component. The descriptive component then states the matter of fact that the predicate corresponds to, and the attitudinal component expresses an "attitude" (an emotion or volition) exactly as in noncognitivist accounts of the function of "good," "ought," and so on.

Hare's argument for the claim that "rude" is not a normative word at all was the following: Hare first cites an example from Lawrence Kohlberg in which a boy spits in the face of another boy while both are sitting in a classroom.[15] The victim "quietly slugged the other without leaving his seat." The teacher noticed, and the boy said, "Teacher, I hit him because he spit in my face." The teacher replied, "That wasn't polite, it was rude." As the children went back to work, the boy who had done the slugging said to his opponent with a grin, "I will grant you that, it was rude."

Hare's comment is, "I hope this case will convince Mrs. Foot that it is possible to accept that an act satisfies the descriptive conditions for being called 'rude' without being committed to evaluating it adversely, even though 'rude' is normally an adjective of adverse evaluation."

The position Hare defends is that a genuine "adjective of evaluation," that is an adjective whose semantic content is that something possesses intrinsic value (or disvalue), is such that anyone who uses such an adjective without hypocrisy or insincerity must be *motivated* to approve (or disapprove) of it.[16] But, as Elizabeth Anderson has remarked,

> Hare's motivational requirement is unreasonable. For something to count as an authentic value judgment or reason, it must be reflectively endorsable. But actual motivational states are not always

reflectively endorsable. One of the functions of value judgments is to note when one's motivational states are deficient because they fail to track what one judges to be good. Boredom, weakness, apathy, self-contempt, despair and other motivational states can make a person fail to desire what she judges to be good or desire what she judges to be bad. This prevents the identification of value judgments with expressions of actual desires and preferences, as Hare insists.[17]

In addition, Hare ignores the possibility that one can say that something has value (positive or negative) but that value is *outweighed* by something else. Thus, the boy in the example could, if he grew up to be a moral philosopher, defend what he said by saying: "Of course, I was not denying that there is something wrong about rudeness. What I was implying was that it is sometimes *right* to be rude because the person one is rude to has done something to deserve it." It is because "rude" has evaluative force that the remark that it is sometimes right to be rude is worth making, while the remark that, "It is sometimes right to go to a restaurant" is not.

When it comes to the word "cruel," however, Hare seems to favor a "two-components" analysis. He recognizes, indeed, that this notion has been regarded as a case of what I am calling "entanglement," but his description of what the proponents of entanglement believe is distorted by a curious projection of his own views onto his opponents. He writes, "It is being suggested that this kind of action is somehow *inherently* motivational; if it did not motivate us in this way, or otherwise touch our feelings, it would not be *that* kind of action (not, for example, cruel). So there are properties that are in themselves evil, and moral words that are inseparably descriptive and prescriptive."[18]

But, as I just noted, proponents of entanglement do not maintain that evaluative words, either thick or thin, satisfy Hare's motivational requirement (which is, basically, that the words in question behave as emotivists claim they do).[19] What they maintain is that if one did not at any point share the relevant ethical point of view one would never be able to acquire a thick ethical concept, and that sophisticated use of such a concept requires a continuing ability to identify (at least in imagination) with that point of view. This is not to deny that someone may know that something is cruel and not be motivated to refrain from it; indeed, someone may know that something is *evil* and not be motivated to refrain from it! After the remark quoted above, however, Hare goes on to argue that "the fact that *if* we use this word we are almost [sic] committed to the evaluation does not entail that we have got to use the word at all in order to describe the action fully. We can say, 'He was caused to suffer deeply,' but add, 'all the same there was nothing wrong in it. . . .'" Here, Hare seems to suggest that the descriptive component of "cruel" is "causing to suffer deeply" and the evaluative "almost" implication is "action that is wrong."

Whether Hare himself means to endorse this "two-components" approach, the whole idea of factorability has been, I believe, effectively criticized, both by myself,[20] by John McDowell,[21] and earlier by Iris Murdoch.[22] The attempt of noncognitivists to split thick ethical concepts into a "descriptive meaning component" and a "prescriptive meaning component" founders on the impossibility of saying what the "descriptive meaning" of, say, "cruel" is without using the word "cruel" or a synonym. For example, it certainly is not the case that the extension of "cruel" (setting the evaluation aside, as it were) is simply "causing deep suffering," *nor*, as Hare himself should have noticed, is "causes deep suffering" itself free of evaluative force. "Suffering" does not just mean "pain," nor does "deep" just mean "a lot of." Before the introduction of anesthesia at the end of the nineteenth century, any operation caused great pain, but the surgeons were not normally being *cruel*, and behavior that does not cause obvious pain at all may be extremely cruel. Imagine that a person debauches a young person with the deliberate aim of keeping him or her from fulfilling some great talent! Even if the victim never feels obvious pain, this may be extremely cruel. As McDowell puts it,

. . . It seems reasonable to be sceptical about whether the disentangling manoeuvre here envisaged [factoring into a descriptive and a prescriptive component] can always be effected; specifically, about whether, corresponding to any value concept, one can always isolate a genuine feature of the world—by the appropriate standard of genuineness [that is, the noncognitivist's]: that is, a feature that is there anyway, independently of anyone's value experience being as it is—to be that to which competent users of the concept are to be regarded as responding when they use it: that which is left in the world when one peels off the reflection of the appropriate attitude.[23]

As I mentioned, John Mackie also considered the word "cruel." He argued that the whole idea of value properties must be wrong, because of the "queerness" that such properties would exhibit,[24] and wrote,

> Another way of bringing out this queerness is to ask, about anything that is supposed to have some objective moral quality, how this is linked with its natural features. What is the connection between the *natural fact* that an action is a piece of deliberate cruelty—say causing pain just for fun—and the moral fact that it is wrong? . . . It is not even sufficient to postulate a faculty which "sees" the wrongness: something must be postulated which can see at once *the natural features that constitute the cruelty,* and the wrongness, and the *mysterious consequential link between the two.*"[25] (Emphasis added.)

Hare saw that thick ethical concepts pose a problem and tried to respond to it; Mackie was simply blind to the problem. For Mackie, "cruel" (and presumably Hume's example "crime") were just words that describe "natural facts." But *what sort* of "natural facts"?

What is characteristic of "negative" descriptions like "cruel," as well as of "positive" descriptions like "brave," "temperate," and "just" (note that these are the terms that Socrates keeps forcing his interlocutors to discuss again and again) is that to use them with any discrimination one has to be able to identify imaginatively with an *evaluative point of view.* That is why someone who thought that "brave" simply meant "not afraid to risk life and limb" would not be able to understand the all-important distinction that Socrates keeps drawing between mere *rashness* or *foolhardiness* and genuine *bravery*. It is also the reason that (as Iris Murdoch stressed in a wonderful book, *The Sovereignty of Good*) it is always possible to *improve one's understanding* of a concept like "impertinence" or "cruelty." This dependence of even "descriptive" uses of "cruel" upon evaluation is what Mackie was *denying* when he referred to the fact that someone is cruel as simply a (metaphysically unproblematic) "natural fact."

As I explained in the preceding chapter, for the empiricists a "fact" was, at bottom, simply something one could have a "sense impression" of (or, in the subjective idealist version defended by Berkeley and flirted with by Hume, a fact was simply a complex of sense qualities). This crude empiricist criterion was replaced in the twentieth century by the various versions of the Verifiability Theory of Meaning developed by logical positivists. But the collapse of the various grounds on which the fact/value dichotomy was originally defended, including the Verifiability Theory of Meaning, has not led to a demise of the dichotomy, even among professional philosophers. What it has led to is a change in the nature of the *arguments* offered for the dichotomy. Today it is defended more and more on metaphysical grounds. At the same time, even the defenders of the dichotomy concede that the old arguments for the dichotomy were bad arguments.[26]

The most common metaphysical ground is simply *physicalism*. The most sophisticated versions—for example, Bernard Williams's version—do not claim that we can *in practice* get along with a vocabulary consisting of the sorts of terms that figure in our most fundamental science (which the defenders of these versions take to be physics).[27] Nevertheless, the world as it is in itself, independent of all observers, can be described using only such scientific terms, according to Williams. A fact, in what Williams calls an "absolute" sense, is something that can be described in the vocabulary that science is destined to "converge" upon in its indefinitely continued inquiry. And we know what that vocabulary will be: it will be the vocabulary of (an improved and perfected) *physics*, a physics that describes the world in terms of *primary qualities alone*. Thus Williams writes: "The world itself has only *primary* qualities."[28] And he writes:

> The roughly Peircean conception I have sketched involves at most an ideal limit of certainty as the *end* of scientific enquiry, that "fixation of belief" to which such enquiry tends. It in no way involves certainty as the point from which such an enquiry must set out, nor as a point which we must suppose it to have already reached, nor need we think that our present physical conceptions are adequate or unshakeable. To suppose, on the other hand, that we have no conception at all of what an adequate physics might look like would hopelessly weaken these notions—even the notion of an absolute conception, so to speak, would look too pale if we accepted that.[29]

Note how "absolute conception of the world" and "adequate physics" are identified in this passage. What follows from Williams's metaphysical story is, however, not a *fact/value* dichotomy at all, but rather a dichotomy between what is "absolutely" the case, true independently of the perspective of any observer, and what is only true relative to one or another "perspective." Williams, for example, does not deny that ethical sentences can be true or false; what he denies is that they can be true or false *nonperspectivally*. Thus the position Williams defends has been renamed: instead of "noncognitivism" it is called "relativism." The slogan is that ethical sentences can be true, but not "absolutely" so; they are only true relative to "some social world or other."[30] According to Williams, "Peter is cruel" can be true in the very same sense in which "Grass is green" is true, while still being an ethical utterance. The point is that for Williams *factual statements* in a natural language like "Grass is green" are not treated as possessing the highest kind of truth. If I say that grass is green, for example, I certainly speak the truth; but I do not speak what he calls the *absolute* truth. I do not describe the world as it is "anyway," independent of any and every "perspective." The concept "green" and possibly the concept "grass" as well are not concepts that "the absolute conception of the world" would use to describe the properties that things have apart from any "local perspective."[31]

As Vivian Walsh sums it up (referring both to Williams's views and to my published criticisms of those views):[32]

> So, according to the new dichotomists, we are to wait around for finished science to tell us (presumably in a constructed language which it endorses) what things are absolutely true. Putnam does not mince words: "This dichotomy between what the world is like independent of any local perspective and what is projected by us seems to me utterly indefensible."[33] . . .
>
> The would be "positive" economist [and the would-be "positive" lawyer as well, I might add—HP] is unlikely to be cheered up by being offered a dichotomy that rests, not just on a metaphysical argument, but on a demonstrably bad metaphysical argument. But there is a more work-a-day objection that may be even more telling. Economists [and lawyers as well, I add—HP] cannot afford to neglect the failure of an advertising campaign that tried to sell a shade of green which consumers rejected, or the devastating results of a record drought upon grasslands. The things consumers [and clients] want, or buy, or have produced for them, are chosen or rejected in terms of features that arguably would not appear in "completed science" if it should ever arrive. They live, move, and have their being, just like those who make moral statements, on the "wrong" side of the dichotomy between "finished science" and *everything else that anyone ever says.*

Mackie, who, like Williams, was attracted to a physicalist account of facts, attempted to exploit a property that he claimed ethical judgments possess: that one cannot make an ethical judgment, and mean it *as* a sincere ethical judgment, unless one thereby expresses an *actual* desire or preference. Since descriptions of fact cannot, according to Mackie, be expressions of actual desires and preferences, it follows that ethical judgments are not descriptions of fact, Q.E.D.

But the origin of this supposed property of ethical judgments is clear: it comes from the older *emotivism* of the logical positivists! For the logical positivists and their emotivist followers expressing actual desires and preferences was the very "function" of ethical judgments. However, as Elizabeth Anderson points out in the passage I quoted earlier (and as has been recognized as far back as Aristotle's writings about *akrasia,* or weakness of will), there are many reasons why I may sincerely believe that something is good and *not* be motivated to desire or choose it.

Mackie did not, however, follow the emotivists in concluding that ethical judgments *are,* semantically speaking, expressions of desire and preference. Rather, he adopted his famous "error theory" according to which "good" *means* a property that is supposed to be such that the knowledge that something has it *necessarily* motivates the person who has that knowledge to desire or prefer it. Since there cannot be such a property (according to Mackie), every time we say that something is "good" we are making an *error* (a metaphysical error, in fact: attributing to something a *metaphysically absurd property*).[34] The reason I nevertheless attribute to Mackie an emotivist influence is that his argument for the metaphysical absurdity of goodness rests on his *description* of how the word "good" is used, and *that* description was (like Hare's) strongly influenced by emotivism.

Few if any contemporary philosophers have accepted Mackie's "error theory," however. The positions that are still defended by the proponents of a fact/value dichotomy are variants of noncognitivism and relativism. But noncognitivism founders, as we have seen, once we appreciate what I have been calling *the entanglement of fact and value,* while the relativism derived from contemporary scientism threatens to toss much more than ethical judgments into the bag of truths that are only valid from some "local perspective" or other.

WHY ARE WE TEMPTED BY THE FACT/VALUE DICHOTOMY?

There are a variety of reasons why we are tempted to draw a line between "facts" and "values"—and to draw it in such a way that "values" are put outside the realm of rational argument altogether. For one thing, it is much easier to say, "that's a value judgment," meaning, "that's just a matter of subjective preference," than to do what Socrates tried to teach us: to examine who we are and what our deepest convictions are and hold those convictions up to the searching test of reflective examination. As Michele Moody-Adams argued in an important book about cultural relativism, if we give up the very idea of a "rationally irresolvable" ethical dispute, we are not thereby committing ourselves to the prospect of actually resolving all our ethical disagreements, but we *are* committing ourselves to the idea that there is always the possibility of further discussion and further examination of any disputed issue, including the Socratic self-examination that I just spoke of.[35] The worst thing about the fact/value dichotomy is that in practice it functions as a discussion-stopper, and not just a discussion-stopper, but a thought-stopper. But there are less disreputable reasons for being attracted to relativism, noncognitivism, the error theory, and the like, and the other contemporary versions of the dichotomy.

One reason, Bernard Williams's reason, is that he does not see how to provide us with a *metaphysical explanation of the possibility of ethical knowledge*. This metaphysical cum epistemological appeal is one I think we should resist. It is not that I possess a metaphysical story that explains how I know, for example, that concern for the welfare of others regardless of national, ethnic, or religious boundaries, and freedom of speech and thought are better than the alternatives except in the sense of being able to offer the sorts of arguments that ordinary nonmetaphysical people with liberal convictions can and do offer. The very idea of explaining how ethical knowledge is possible in "absolute" terms seems to me ridiculous. As Williams admits, it seems impossible to explain in "absolute" terms how "content" is possible—that is, how *thought, belief,* and *reference* are possible.[36] But to say that we only *think* that we think is absurd (even if certain continental thinkers might be happy with this suggestion). Indeed, the long history of failures to explain in metaphysical terms how mathematics is possible, how nondemonstrative knowledge is possible (the so-called "problem of induction"), and so on, suggests that nothing much follows from the failure of philosophy to come up with an explanation of *anything* in "absolute terms"—except, perhaps, the senselessness of a certain sort of metaphysics.

Another, still more respectable appeal is to those who fear that the alternative to cultural relativism is cultural imperialism. But recognizing that our judgments claim objective validity and recognizing that they are shaped by a particular culture and by a particular problematic situation are not incompatible. And this is true of scientific questions as well as ethical ones. The solution is neither to give up on the very possibility of rational discussion nor to seek an Archimedean point, an "absolute conception" outside of all contexts and problematic situations, but—as Dewey taught his whole life long—to investigate and discuss and try things out cooperatively, democratically, and above all *fallibilistically*.

TILL NEXT TIME . . .

In these two chapters I have tried to show just how poor the arguments for the fact/value dichotomy are (and have always been), and how the important phenomenon (or rather, phenomena) of fact/value entanglement everywhere subvert that dichotomy. So far, the discussion has been abstract. In order to bring it down to earth, and to see some of the real world issues that come into view when we abandon the dichotomy, in my next chapter I shall examine the intellectual career and contribution of a great economist-philosopher, Amartya Sen, with the purpose of seeing how the very nature of "classical theory" in economics becomes transformed in his work and how that transformation is directly connected with the issues that I have been discussing.

3 | FACT AND VALUE IN THE WORLD OF AMARTYA SEN

The support that believers in, and advocates of, self-interested behavior have sought in Adam Smith is, in fact, hard to find on a wider and less biased reading of Smith. The professor of moral philosophy and the pioneer economist did not, in fact, lead a life of spectacular schizophrenia. Indeed, it is precisely the narrowing of the broad Smithian view of human beings, in modern economics, that can be seen as one of the major deficiencies of modern economic theory. This impoverishment is closely related to the distancing of economics from ethics.

—AMARTYA SEN

IN THE PRECEDING CHAPTERS I criticized the arguments for the fact/value dichotomy. I showed, first, that both historically and conceptually those arguments originated in an impoverished empiricist (and later an equally impoverished logical positivist) conception of fact, and second, that if we do not see that facts and values are deeply "entangled" we shall misunderstand the nature of fact as badly as logical positivists misunderstood the nature of value. In this chapter (as I have promised) I shall relate these issues to the work of Amartya Sen, work that has transformed our understanding of what "classical economic theory" was about in addition to having important implications for questions of global welfare. The value of Amartya Sen's contribution is, of course, widely recognized (as the award of a Nobel Prize in economics in 1998 confirms). Although this would have been my plan in any case, I note the pleasant coincidence that Sen was also the Rosenthal Lecturer in 1998!

SEN, ADAM SMITH, AND "SECOND PHASE" CLASSICAL ECONOMICS

> We can say by twisting Shakespeare a little, that while some men are
> born small and some achieve smallness, Adam Smith has had much
> smallness thrust upon him.
> —AMARTYA SEN[1]

Vivian Walsh, who, like Amartya Sen, is both a moral philosopher
and an economist,[2] has recently traced the development of what he
calls "the revival of classical [economic] theory during the twentieth century" with special attention to Amartya Sen's place in what
Walsh sees as the emerging "second phase" of that theory.[3] He begins his narrative by pointing out that the "habit of concentration
on a few key issues of classical theory" was a prominent feature of
the work of the theorists who initiated the revival of classical economics at the beginning of the twentieth century, "and their main
preoccupation was naturally with Ricardo."[4]

As Walsh has noted elsewhere, Ricardo himself never lost sight
of the deep moral implications of Smith's analytical contribution.[5]
But Ricardo knew that he was not a trained moral philosopher, and
so (as he himself tells us)[6] he "confined his attention to those pas-
sages in the writing of Adam Smith from which he sees reason to
differ." Walsh points out that this "Ricardian minimalism" was a no-
table characteristic of the work of Piero Sraffa, von Neumann, and
others, but this is not a criticism of Sraffa or von Neumann or their
contemporaries. As Walsh says, "In fact such a minimalism re-
flected the most critical need for the revival of classical theory: the
most precise possible mathematical development of the structure
of the theory."[7] A similar point is made by Sen himself (note that
Sen's term for what Walsh calls "minimalism" is "the engineering
approach"): "There are many issues on which economics has been
able to provide better understanding and illumination precisely because of the extensive use of the engineering approach."[8] Sen characteristically adds that "these contributions have been made *despite*
the neglect of the ethical approach, since there are important

economic logistic issues that do call for attention, and which can be tackled with efficiency, up to a point, even within the limited format of a narrowly construed non-ethical view of human motivation and behavior." (Sen gives as an illustration the development of general equilibrium theory, which, he says, brings out "important interrelations that call for technical analysis of a high order.")

If it was important in the twentieth century to perfect the mathematical tools of the "minimalist" approach, Sen insists that something additional is needed now. "The impoverishment of welfare economics related to its distancing from ethics," he writes, "affects both *welfare economics* (narrowing its reach and relevance) and *predictive economics* (weakening its behavioral foundations)."[9] However, if we are to understand Sen's place in history, the reintroduction of ethical concerns and concepts into economic discourse must not be thought of as an *abandonment* of "classical economics"; rather it is a *reintroduction* of something that was everywhere present in the writings of Adam Smith and that went hand-in-hand with Smith's technical analyses. This is something that Sen himself stresses; again and again he points out that Adam Smith is being misrepresented by those who would construe him as the prophet of "economic man." Those who see Smith in such a way are fond of quoting the following passage: "It is not from the benevolence of the butcher, the brewer, or the baker that we expect our dinner, but from their regard to their own interest. We address ourselves, not to their humanity but to their self-love, and never talk to them of our own necessities but of their advantages."[10] Sen's dry comment on this use of the passage is:

> While many admirers of Smith do not seem to have gone beyond this bit about the butcher and the brewer, a reading of even this passage would indicate that what Smith is doing here is to specify why and how normal transactions in the market are carried out, and why and how division of labour works, which is the subject of the chapter in which the quoted passage occurs. But the fact that Smith noted that mutually advantageous trades are very common does not

indicate at all that he thought that self-love . . . could be adequate for a good society. Indeed, he maintained precisely the opposite. He did not rest economic salvation on some unique motivation.[11]

Walsh's term "second phase classical theory" is thus the right term for the Senian program. That program involves introducing ethical concerns and concepts into economics without sacrificing the rigorous tools contributed by "first phase" theory.

ETHICS AND ECONOMICS

In *Ethics and Economics* as well as in his many papers and lectures, Sen has sought to challenge standard economists' picture of (1) what economic rationality requires; (2) what the motivations of economic actors can realistically be assumed to be; and (3) what criteria of economic performance and social well-being welfare economics can legitimately use.[12] In addition, he has not only enriched our understanding of such tragic phenomena as *famine* and the millions of "missing women" (that is, the shorter life-expectancies of women as compared with men in large parts of the world), but he has also proposed a positive approach to the evaluation of well-being, the "capabilities approach."

I shall say something about each of these, and then close by connecting my discussion to the topics in the first two chapters.

(1) Does One Have to Be Selfish to Be Rational?

"How is rational behavior characterized in standard economic theory? It is fair to say that there are two predominant methods of defining rationality of behavior in mainline economic theory. One is to see rationality as internal *consistency* of choice and the other is to identify rationality with *maximization of self-interest*."[13]

Amartya Sen has written extensively on questions concerning the notions of consistency of both preferences and choices (and the relation between choices and preferences).[14] But quite apart from the question as to just how these consistency notions are to be interpreted mathematically (and the important question as to whether the notion of *purely internal consistency* is itself cogent), the idea that internal consistency of choice can be a sufficient condition of rationality seems absurd, as Sen notes.[15] Once we give up the idea—itself the product of a narrow verificationism that is a hangover of logical positivism—that one's choices must flawlessly "reveal" one's values, it is impossible to avoid the question of the relation of a person's choices to his or her values, as well as the question of the evaluation of those values themselves. The idea that only *self-interested* values are "rational" is even harder to defend. In part the prestige of this idea in economics derives from the false supposition that it is what Adam Smith taught, an idea that, as we have already seen, depends on a misreading of Smith that Sen has repeatedly and consistently tried to correct.

(2) The Motivations of Economic Actors

Often economists defend the strategy of assuming that economic actors are "rational" as what Sen calls an "intermediary" strategy: actual behavior is identified with rational behavior, on the ground (or methodological hope) that actual behavior is close enough to rational for this "simplifying" assumption to work, and then rational behavior is assumed to be identical with self-interested behavior. Sen's uncharacteristically savage comment is as follows:

> The complex procedure of equating self-interest with rationality and then identifying actual behavior with rational behavior seems to be thoroughly counterproductive if the ultimate intention is to provide a reasonable case for the assumption of self-interest maximization in the specification of *actual* behavior in economic theory. To try to use the demands of rationality in going to battle on behalf of the standard behavioral assumption of economic theory (to wit, *actual* self-interest maximization) is like leading a cavalry charge on a lame donkey.[16]

The assumption that people act only on self-interested motives was sometimes defended on the basis of the hedonist psychology of Jeremy Bentham, the father of utilitarianism, which held that everyone ultimately "really" desires only a subjective psychological quantity (called "pleasure" by Bentham) and that this "quantity" was a purely *subjective* matter. As John Dewey put it long ago, "When happiness is conceived of as an aggregate of states of feeling, these are regarded as homogenous in quality, different from one another only in intensity and duration. Their qualitative differences are not intrinsic, but are due to the different objects with which they are associated (as pleasures of hearing, or vision). Hence they disappear when the pleasure is taken by itself as an end."[17] This disappearance of the qualitative differences is (as far as importance to the agent's "happiness" is concerned), of course, just what makes it possible for the utilitarian to speak of "summing" pleasures, "maximizing" them, and so on. But if Dewey's alternative view is right (as I believe), and if "agreeableness is precisely the agreeableness or congruence of some objective condition with some impulse, habit, or tendency of the agent," then "of course, pure pleasure is a myth. Any pleasure is qualitatively unique, being precisely the harmony of one set of conditions with its appropriate activity. The pleasure of eating is one thing; the pleasure of hearing music, another; the pleasure of an amiable act, another; the pleasure of drunkenness or of anger is still another."[18] Dewey continues, "Hence the possibility of absolutely different moral values attaching to pleasures, according to the type or aspect of character which they express. But if the good is only a sum of pleasures, any pleasure, so far as it goes, is as good as any other—the pleasure of malignity as good as the pleasure of kindness, simply as pleasure."[19]

Dewey not only anticipates the point made by Nozick with the aid of his famous thought experiment of the "experience machine" that what we want in life is not mere feelings (otherwise we would all choose to spend our lives in the experience machine) but rather the objective fulfillment of desires, capacities, and efforts, but he also anticipates Nozick's point that "what *we are* is important to us."[20] As Dewey also writes, "Not only the 'good,' but the more vigorous and hearty of the 'bad,' would scorn a life in which character, selfhood, had no significance, and where the experimental discovery and testing of destiny had no place."[21]

Sen argues in a number of places that people are very often powerfully moved, not only by motives other than subjective "pleasure," but by a great variety of non-self-interested motives—not only ethical motives, although there is no reason for refusing to recognize that these may be powerful in certain circumstances, but also loyalties of all kinds, both good and bad, both to ideas and to groups (as well as group hatreds of all kinds).

Last but not least, not only are people not simply motivated by self-interest, but even more disastrously for the way the notion of "self-interest" is often used by the economists Sen criticizes, there is an enormous difference between maximizing genuine long-term self-interest (which is usually *not* what is understood by the term "self-interest") and maximizing mere short-term self-interest. When this is seen, it becomes clear that the modern version of "economic man" is neither genuinely rational nor truly acting in his or her self-interest.

(3) Criteria of Economic Performance and Social Well-Being

During the Great Depression a rather remarkable change took place in welfare economics. To understand this change, we need to recall a bit of history.

Some economists started using the concept of utility in the eighteenth century, and by the end of the nineteenth century it had achieved a particular form, which became virtually standard. It was assumed by the "neo-classical" economists (William Stanley Jevons, Alfred Marshall, and their followers) that there was something called "utility," which could be quantified. (Edgeworth's brilliant—and preposterous at least by present standards—*Mathematical Psychics*, published in 1881, and repeatedly republished thereafter, assumed a unit of utility called the "Util.") "Utility curves" were plotted, which showed how utility supposedly increased with increasing quantities of a given commodity. These curves assumed a particular shape, a shape governed by what was called the Law of Diminishing Marginal Utility. According to this "law," the marginal utility (the utility of the last amount consumed) decreases with additional consumption. (Alfred Marshall illustrated this with the charming example of a small boy eating berries.)

Arthur Cecil Pigou's enormously influential *Economics of Welfare*, published in 1920, derived a simple argument for at least some redistribution of wealth from these "neo-classical" premises. If the Law of Diminishing Marginal Utility is right, then the marginal utility of *money* should also diminish. And even if these marginal utilities vary considerably from person to person, it is still plausible that the marginal utility of, say, a thousand dollars to someone at the point of going hungry or becoming a homeless beggar is much greater than the marginal utility of a thousand dollars to, say, Bill Gates. Conclusion: the total utility (often identified with "the total happiness" by utilitarian writers) of the population as a whole would be increased by taking a thousand dollars away from Bill Gates in taxes and giving a thousand dollars to the destitute person; more generally, *other things being equal, income redistribution promotes welfare.*

Interestingly enough, it was during the depths of the Depression that Lionel Robbins, certainly one of the most influential economists in the world, persuaded the entire economics profession that *interpersonal comparisons of utility are "meaningless."*[22] Although these views were not the product of logical positivism (Walsh has pointed out that at the beginning of the 1930s Robbins seems to have been influenced by Jevons's skepticism concerning the possibility of knowledge of the states of mind of other people—a skepticism that is contrary to the behaviorist doctrines of logical positivism), by 1935, Robbins was beginning to be influenced by logical positivism as well.[23] In particular, he held strong views to the effect that rational discussion ("argument") is impossible in ethics, and therefore ethical questions must be kept wholly out of economics. With one stroke, the idea that the economist could and should be concerned with the welfare of the society in an evaluative sense was rejected, and in its place was inserted the positivist idea that such a concern was "meaningless," at least from a scientific point of view. A couple of quotations from Robbins will give the flavor of the idea:

> If we disagree about ends it is a case of thy blood or mine—or live or let live according to the importance of the difference, or the relative strength of our opponents. But if we disagree about means, then scientific analysis can often help us resolve our differences. If we disagree about the morality of the taking of interest (and we understand what we are talking about), then there is no room for argument.[24]

And again: "It does not seem logically possible to associate the two studies [ethics and economics] in any form but mere juxtaposition. Economics deals with ascertainable facts; ethics with valuation and obligations."[25]

After they had been persuaded to accept these views by Lionel Robbins (later Lord Lionel Robbins), economists did not simply conclude that there was no such field as "welfare economics." Instead they looked (strange as this may sound) for a *value neutral criterion of optimal economic functioning*. And they found one, or so they believed, in the notion of "Pareto optimality."

Recall that utility itself had not been declared a "meaningless" notion. Indeed, a theorem proved by von Neumann to the effect that (in the case of one single consumer) any formally consistent set of choices could be "represented" mathematically by a function assigning utilities to the various "bundles" of commodities (that is, to the possible combinations of choices) seemed to justify speaking "as if" there were such a thing as "utility" without having to make any of the heavy philosophical assumptions that went with the use of that notion in the nineteenth century (for example, the assumption that "utility" is a mental quality of some kind, or the assumption that it is—or isn't—the same as "pleasure"). (I have criticized the assumptions needed for the proof of this theorem, however, and so have Sen and numerous others.)[26] What *had* been declared to be meaningless was not "utility" but *intersubjective comparison of utilities.*

I pause to note that while the utilitarians' assumptions about "utility" were in many ways absurd, and while the idea that the amount of satisfaction different people get from various goods and services (and from such intangibles as *opportunities*) can be linearly ordered also seems absurd, the idea that there is a *partial ordering* here is not at all absurd. To revert to my example above (the one derived from Pigou), the idea that a thousand dollars matters almost not at all to Bill Gates and matters enormously to someone who is about to lose the roof over his or her head, is not at all absurd. Again, one does not need to suppose that welfare is simply a function of monetary income, an assumption that Sen has repeatedly criticized, to think there is *some* validity to the Pigou argument for a certain amount of income redistribution. Speaking of the problem of assigning "weights" to the various factors that one might count as contributing (positively or negatively) to welfare, Sen has written:

> It is of course crucial to ask, in any evaluative exercise of this kind, how the weights are to be selected. This judgmental exercise can be resolved only through reasoned evaluation. For a particular person, who his making his or her own judgments, the selection of weights will require reflection, rather than any interpersonal agreement (or consensus). However, in arriving at an "agreed" range for *social evaluation* (for example in social studies of poverty), there has to be some kind of a reasoned "consensus" on weights, or at least on a range of weights. This is a "social choice" exercise, and it requires public discussion and a democratic understanding and acceptance.[27]

What the positivist views that came to dominate economic

thinking did was to proscribe the very idea of a "reasoned" consensus on any value question. If value questions are questions of "thy blood or mine," the very notion of reason makes no sense: "there is no room for argument."

Pareto optimality is, however, a terribly weak criterion for evaluating socioeconomic states of affairs. Defeating Nazi Germany in 1945 could not be called Pareto optimal, for example, because at least one agent—Adolf Hitler—was moved to a lower utility surface.[28] Moreover, if the reason for favoring Pareto optimality as a criterion is that one approves of the underlying value judgment that every agent's right to maximize his or her utility is as important as every other's, then it would seem that Pareto optimality isn't a *value neutral* criterion of "optimality" at all. How could there be a *value neutral* criterion of *optimality*, anyway?

The upshot of this little bit of history is that if there is to be such a subject as welfare economics at all, and in particular, if welfare economics is to speak to problems of poverty and other forms of deprivation, then welfare economics cannot avoid substantive ethical questions. Yet, if we cannot simply go back to nineteenth-century utilitarianism, nor (Sen has argued) accept twentieth-century versions of utilitarianism, what is the alternative?[29] This is the question to which Sen has devoted a remarkable series of books and lectures.

THE CAPABILITIES APPROACH

The approach that Amartya Sen has elaborated and argued for in the works to which I just referred is called the "capabilities approach." The "capabilities" that Sen speaks of are particularly capabilities "to achieve functionings that [a person] has reason to value, and this yields a particular way of viewing the assessment of equality and inequality."[30] Sen explains, "The functionings included can vary from the most elementary ones, such as being well-nourished, avoiding escapable morbidity and premature mortality, etc., to quite complex and sophisticated achievements, such as having self-respect, being able to take part in the life of the community, and so on."[31]

Since I have referred repeatedly to the work of Vivian Walsh, it is appropriate to mention that this notion of "functionings" was anticipated by Walsh in 1961 in *Scarcity and Evil*. Walsh's term was "achievements," and like Sen he connected a very wide notion of achievements or functionings with a concern for the character of a human life as a whole, which goes back to Aristotle. The idea of applying this point of view to problems of *development* is, of course, due entirely to Sen. In recent years, Martha Nussbaum has also used a "capabilities" approach to discuss development issues, particularly as they affect women.[32]

Obviously I do not have the time to explain the capability approach in detail, much less to discuss the rival approaches to questions of poverty, welfare, and global justice that Sen considers and rejects (for example, Rawlsian liberalism, Nozickian libertarianism, and the several versions of utilitarianism). But that is not necessary for my purpose, which is to see how welfare economics has found itself forced to recognize that its "classical" concern with economic well-being (and its opposite, economic deprivation) is essentially a moral concern and cannot be addressed responsibly as long as we are unwilling to take reasoned moral argument seriously.

Precisely because Sen's concerns as an economist are frequently, in fact characteristically, international in scope, his writing often addresses problems of what is called "economic development." In this area, the conventional wisdom is that the sole problem is to raise the monetary income or perhaps the gross economic output of "underdeveloped" nations. One way in which Sen shows us the need for more sensitive measures of "underdevelopment," poverty, and other forms of economic deprivation is by observing how feeble a measure of economic well-being money and gross economic product are by themselves, and how seriously our "information base" is restricted when we fail to gather information about what results flow from given levels of income or production under various conditions.[33] As Sen continues:

> The relationship between income and capability [is] strongly affected by the age of the person (e.g. by the specific needs of the very old and the very young), by gender and social roles (e.g. through special responsibilities of maternity and also custom-determined family obligations), by location (e.g. by the proneness to flooding or drought, or by insecurity and violence in some inner-city living), by epidemiological atmosphere (e.g. through diseases endemic in a region), and by other variations over which a person may have no—or only limited—control.

A striking statistic that Sen uses to illustrate this point is the following:

> Men in China and in Kerala decisively outlive African American men in terms of surviving to older age groups. Even African American women end up having a survival pattern for the higher ages similar to the much poorer Chinese, and decidedly lower survival rates than the even poorer Indians in Kerala. So it is not only the case that American blacks suffer from *relative* deprivation in terms of income per head vis-à-vis American whites, they are also *absolutely* more deprived than the low income Indians in Kerala (for both women and men), and the Chinese (in the case of men), in terms of living to ripe old ages.[34]

As I said, I do not have time to discuss the several versions of utilitarianism, but I do want to call attention to *one* interesting criticism that Sen makes of a particular version of utilitarianism, the version according to which well-being can be measured simply by *desire* satisfaction.[35] The novel point that Sen makes is that in cases of extreme and long-lasting deprivation, the satisfaction of desires can also be an impoverished information base because a frequent consequence of this sort of deprivation is the reduction in the range of desires owing to the hopelessness of the situation. As Sen writes:

> The problem is particularly acute in the context of entrenched inequalities and deprivations. A thoroughly deprived person, leading

a very reduced life, might not appear to be badly off in terms of the mental metric of desire and its fulfillment, if the hardship is accepted with non-grumbling resignation. In situations of long-standing deprivation, the victims do not go on grieving and lamenting all the time, and very often make great efforts to take pleasure in small mercies and to cut down personal desires to modest—"realistic"—proportions. . . . The extent of a person's deprivation may not at all show up in the metric of desire-fulfillment, even though he or she may be quite unable to be adequately nourished, decently clothed, minimally educated, and properly sheltered.[36]

"Capabilities," in Sen's sense, are not simply valuable functionings; they are *freedoms* to enjoy valuable functionings, a point that is announced in the title of Sen's recent book *Development as Freedom* and stressed throughout that book. Obviously, there is room for disagreement as to just which functionings are "valuable" or such that people have "reason to value them," but this room for disagreement is something that Sen regards as valuable rather than disadvantageous. Indeed, Sen does not even claim that the capability approach includes *all* the factors one might wish to include in the evaluation of welfare: "we might, for example, attach importance to rules and procedures and not just to freedoms and outcomes."[37] And he asks the question, "Is this plurality an embarrassment for advocacy of the capability perspective for evaluative purposes?" to which he responds with a firm negative:

Quite the contrary. To insist that there should be only one homogeneous magnitude that we value is to reduce drastically the range of our evaluative reasoning. It is not, for example, to the credit of classical utilitarianism that it values only pleasure, without taking any direct interest in freedom, rights, creativity, or actual living conditions. To insist on the mechanical comfort of having just one homogeneous "good thing" would be to deny our humanity as reasoning creatures. It is like seeking to make the life of the chef easier by finding something which—and which *alone*—we all like (such as smoked salmon, or perhaps even french fries), or some one quality which we must all try to maximize (such as the saltiness of the food).[38]

Mathematically speaking, what the capabilities approach yields (even when we have agreed on a list of valuable functionings—something that itself, as Sen has told us, requires "public discussion and a democratic understanding and acceptance") is not a complete ordering of situations with respect to positive welfare, but a partial ordering, and a somewhat fuzzy one at that.[39] The approach (sometimes Sen calls it a "perspective") does not pretend to yield a "decision method" that could be programmed on a computer. What it does do is invite us to think about what functionings form part of our and other cultures' notions of a good life and to investigate just how much freedom to achieve various of those functionings various groups of people in various situations actually have. Such an approach will require us to stop compartmentalizing "ethics" and "economics" and "politics" in the way we have been doing since Lionel Robbins triumphed over the Pigovian welfare economists in 1932, and come back to the kind of reasoned and humane evaluation of social well-being that Adam Smith saw as essential to the task of the economist.

CONCLUSION: ENTANGLEMENT AGAIN

In the first chapter I began by explaining the difference between an ordinary *distinction* and a metaphysical *dichotomy*, using the analytic-synthetic distinction/dichotomy (at different times it was one or the other of these) as an illustration. I pointed out that if the fact/value distinction is intended as a mere distinction, it is not univocal; we get one "partitioning" of the space of judgments if we take value judgments to be judgments in which certain relatively abstract or "thin" ethical concepts figure (for example, "good," "bad," "ought," "should," "duty," "virtue," "obligation," "right," "wrong"), a somewhat different partitioning if we take value judgments to be judgments that praise or blame some person or persons, and we get still other possible interpretations of the distinction.[40] This fuzziness does not, of course, make the distinction unusable. More important, the possibility of distinguishing a class of "value judgments" in one way or another does not, by itself, have any implications at all as to whether value judgments can or can not be *true or false, justified or unjustified*, do or do not have any descriptive content, and so on; nor does it have any implications as to whether the complementary class of *non–value judgments* has any unity at all. When the distinction becomes a dichotomy—perhaps I should have used John Dewey's term, a *dualism*—it typically gets accompanied by a highly contentious set of metaphysical claims (even they are typically claimed to be *anti*-metaphysical claims). The form of the fact/value dichotomy I have been concerned with originated (so I claim) with David Hume and reached the form in which it was so influential in the twentieth century with logical positivism. In that form, the dichotomy was between cognitively meaningless judgments, which included but were not limited to value judgments, and cognitively meaningful judgments. Within the space of cognitively meaningful judgments, in turn, there was a further dichotomy: every cognitively meaningful judgment—that means every judgment that can figure in a rational *argument*—was either analytic or synthetic, either a "tautology" (in which class the positivists included all of mathematics) or a description of some "fact" or possible fact. The latter dichotomy never had either the popular appeal or the influence of the dichotomy between "facts" and "value judgments," perhaps because the question of the status of mathematical judgments has not been one that many people are concerned with, but the idea that "value judgments" are subjective and that there cannot really be reasoned *argument* about values has had widespread influence (as we see, particularly with the example of Lionel Robbins), as has the question, "Is that a fact or a value judgment?" However, the philosophical arguments for the dichotomy all turned on doctrines concerning the nature of "facts," which collapsed in the face of criticisms by Quine and others early in the second half of the twentieth century.

At the close of the first chapter, I argued that the picture of our language in which nothing can be *both* a fact *and* value-laden is wholly inadequate and that an enormous amount of our descriptive vocabulary is and has to be "entangled."

In the second chapter, I considered the way in which noncognitivist philosophers like Hare and Mackie tried to deal with this "entangled" vocabulary. Hare, who is by far the more sophisticated thinker, tried to separate what he called "secondarily evaluative" terms (what I called "thick ethical terms") into a descriptive component and a prescriptive (or imperative) component, but I argued that this attempt was a total failure. I argued (following a lead pioneered by Iris Murdoch and followed by John McDowell, among others) that the ability to make a nuanced and sophisticated use of any one of these terms—for example, to draw the distinction between *courageous* behavior and behavior that is merely *rash* or *foolhardy*, a distinction that is as old as ethics itself—depends precisely on being able to acquire a particular evaluative point of view. "Valuation" and "description" are interdependent—a possibility that is constantly overlooked by positivists and their ilk.

I have shown how the fact/value dichotomy or dualism (in a virulent form in which ethical questions were considered to be questions of "thy blood or mine") penetrated neoclassical economics after 1932, and I have shown the resultant impoverishment of welfare economics' ability to *evaluate* what it was supposed to evaluate, *economic well-being*. I have discussed Amartya Sen's impressive attempt to enrich the evaluative capacity of welfare and developmental economics by means of the "capabilities approach." Let me now make explicit the connection, which I have so far left implicit, between the topics of this chapter and the "abstract" topics of Chapters 1 and 2: the capabilities approach requires that we use the vocabulary that one inevitably uses, the vocabulary that one *must* use, to talk of capabilities in the sense of "capacities for valuable functions," and that vocabulary consists almost entirely of "entangled" concepts, concepts that cannot be simply factored into a "descriptive part" and an "evaluative part." Just about every one of the terms that Sen and his colleagues and followers use when they talk about capabilities—"valuable functioning," "functioning a person *has reason* to value," "well nourished," *"premature* mortality," "self-respect," "able to take part in the life of the community"—is an entangled term. The standpoint that Sen shows we must take if we are to make responsible evaluations in welfare and developmental economics is not the standpoint that says (as Robbins said) that "it does not seem logically possible to associate the two studies [ethics and economics] in any form but mere juxtaposition. Economics deals with ascertainable facts; ethics, with valuation and obligations."[41] It is a standpoint that says that valuation and the "ascertaining" of facts are interdependent activities.

It is ironic that in Europe there was another tradition in the social sciences, one coming from Max Weber, which also sharply separated factual and ethical questions, but which acknowledged a certain interdependence.[42] For Max Weber, the decision as to *what question the social scientist investigates* was and had to be one that involved ethical values. But once the choice was made, the ascertaining of the answer to the scientist's question was not to be dictated by that scientist's value system. With this I am sure Amartya Sen would agree. But what Max Weber failed to acknowledge was that while indeed the answers to a scientific question must never be dictated by one's value system, the terms one uses even in *description* in history and in sociology and the other social sciences are invariably ethically colored; this is nowhere more true than in the case of the terms Weber used to describe his "ideal types."

Two further points emerge from Sen's work that deserve to be emphasized here. First, once one proposes to evaluate economic well-being, one necessarily becomes involved with questions that have been discussed extensively in the literature of ethics. That does not just mean the literature of *utilitarian* ethics (which for many years tended to be the one kind of ethics that economists who did not wish to exclude value judgment altogether regarded as respectable); if it is legitimate for some economists to defend utilitarian measures of well-being, it must be legitimate to consider the arguments against the adequacy of utilitarianism, both in terms of what it allows in its "information base" and in terms of its procedures of evaluation. Moreover, considering arguments against means also considering arguments for *alternatives* to utilitarianism, which is why Sen discusses in detail the work of John Rawls, Robert Nozick, and many others. In short, the serious welfare economists have to have a serious acquaintance with the best of contemporary ethical discussion. (It is not a one-way street; in *Ethics and Economics* Sen argues that ethicists also have much to learn from economics.) Second, it is not only that entangled concepts necessarily figure in *evaluation;* to the extent that people's motivations are significantly influenced by *their* ethical reasoning, we will need to take account of—and to make "descriptive" uses of—a variety of thick ethical concepts in the *description of economically relevant behavior.* As Sen writes, in the concluding paragraph of *Ethics and Economics:*

> I have tried to argue that welfare economics can be substantially enriched by paying more attention to ethics, and that the study of ethics can also benefit from closer contact with economics. I have also argued that even predictive and descriptive economics can be helped by making more room for welfare-economic considerations in the determination of behavior. I have not tried to argue that either of these exercises would be particularly easy. They involve deep-seated ambiguities, and many of the problems are inherently complex. But the case for bringing economics closer to ethics does not rest on this being an easy thing to do. The case lies, instead, on the rewards of the exercise. I have argued that the rewards can be expected to be rather large.[43]

One of the reasons I discussed the fact/value dichotomy in these chapters was not only to provide a philosophical overview of the reasons that made economists like Lionel Robbins think that the development Walsh called "second phase classical economics," the enterprise of "bringing economics closer to ethics," was "logically impossible"; but also, by demolishing those reasons, I wished to provide a philosophy of language that can accommodate and support this second phase. I believe but aware of my own limitations have not tried to document, that very similar issues arise in the law.

II | RATIONALITY AND VALUE

4 | SEN'S "PRESCRIPTIVIST" BEGINNINGS

ONE of the earliest publications by Amartya Sen on moral philosophy is a 1967 essay "The Nature and Classes of Prescriptive Judgments."[1] After reading the account of the overall significance of Sen's work in Chapter 3, one may be surprised to learn that this early essay takes the noncognitivist position of R. M. Hare (which I criticized in Chapter 2) as its starting-point.[2] Yet even at this stage, Sen was chafing at the *implications* of noncognitivism, and this early essay is worth examining for its valiant attempt to reconcile the noncognitivist thesis that value judgments are merely a way of expressing our endorsement of certain imperatives with the claim that it is possible to give *reasons* for and against ethical judgments. It is, I think, worthwhile to examine the distinctions (and even more the *tensions*) in Sen's arguments at this stage in the evolution of his thought.

Hare's best-known statement of his position was set out in *The Language of Morals*.³ Hare subsequently called this position "universal prescriptivism."⁴ He called it "universal" because, according to him, it is a *logical* (that is to say an *analytic*) truth that ethical judgments are universalizable (note how once again the analytic-synthetic dichotomy is being presupposed). If I say that "murder is wrong," then I *must* agree that it is wrong for *anyone* to commit murder if my judgment is to be a truly ethical one. And Hare calls it "prescriptivism" because the value component of an ethical judgment (sometimes Hare uses simply, "value judgment") is properly expressed in the imperative mode. Thus Hare writes, in a passage quoted by Sen: "I propose to say that the test, whether someone is using the judgment 'I ought to do X' as a value judgment or not is, 'Does he or does he not recognize that if he assents to the judgment he must also assent to the command, 'Let me do X?' "⁵ Or as Sen himself put it:

> A value judgment is to be called "purely prescriptive" if by it the author intends to convey only an agreement to the underlying imperative and not any factual information other than that necessary to express the imperative. The factual part consists here only of identifying the alternatives to which the imperative refers. For example, if I say "Capital punishment should be abolished," and mean by it only my agreement to the imperative "Let us abolish capital punishment," this can be taken to be a "purely prescriptive judgment."⁶

It is true that Sen says at the very beginning of this essay that "we shall not enter into the debate whether *all* value judgments are 'prescriptive' or whether *all* of them are 'universalizable'; we shall simply confine our attention to those which have these characteristics, without worrying about whether that leaves some types of value judgments out of consideration."⁷ However, in the course of the article he regularly cites many familiar sorts of "value judgments" as examples, without giving any special argument that they are "prescriptive" in Hare's sense. Evidently, then, at this stage Sen thought that if there *were* other sorts of "value judgments" they could safely be ignored. In addition, the factual information/imperative dichotomy is explicitly presupposed in the passage I just quoted.[8] Finally, a "purely prescriptive" value judgment, that is, one with no descriptive component, conveys *only* an agreement (on the part of the "author" of the value judgment) to an "underlying" imperative. "Capital punishment should be abolished" is "only" a way of conveying the speaker's agreement to the imperative, "Let us abolish capital punishment." How then did Sen find a way to resist the conclusion of the logical positivist A. J. Ayer concerning the relation between a value judgment and its "reasons"? Sen quotes Ayer: "Why people respond favourably to certain facts and unfavourably to others is [merely] a question for the sociologist."[9]

Sen begins with the remark that "one difficulty with Hare's analysis . . . is that while one gets from it a very precise analysis of classes of value *terms* and *expressions*, Hare himself says relatively little on the classes of value *judgments* that use these terms."[10] (In fact, the "analysis of value terms" that Sen referred to here presupposed the doctrine, which I criticized in Part I, of the "factorizability" of value terms into a "prescriptive" and a "descriptive" component.) As Sen explains,[11] "Hare distinguishes between a 'prescriptive term,' which has 'prescriptive meaning,' 'whether or not it has descriptive meaning,' and an 'evaluative term' which has 'both kinds of meaning.'"[12] Sen's strategy in this essay was to "suggest a system of classification of value judgments that corresponds to Hare's general classification of value words," and then to follow this "by introducing two other methods of classification." This was no mere exercise in "classification"; Sen's distinctions, and the discussion that accompanied them, undermine Hare's noncognitivism much more than Sen himself was willing to come out and say (and perhaps more than he himself recognized in 1967).

Sen first distinguished between a "purely prescriptive judgment" (I quoted his definition earlier) and an evaluative judgment, which not only "implies my agreement to an imperative, but also has descriptive content"; this is very much in the spirit of Hare, obviously.

(Sen introduces the symbolic notations J(P) for "purely prescriptive judgment" and J(E) for "evaluative judgment.") His example of an "evaluative judgment," to which I shall return, is the following: "For example, if I say 'Capital punishment is barbarous,' I may try to convey more than my agreement with the imperative quoted earlier (or a modified imperative of a kind to be discussed [in a later section of Sen's paper]), viz. also that capital punishment has certain features usually associated with the notion of barbarity."[13]

Next Sen added an additional and very interesting distinction between what he calls "compulsive and non-compulsive judgments." And finally he reviewed a distinction familiar from both ethics and decision theory, the distinction between "basic" and "non-basic" ends or values.

This whole discussion lies squarely within the framework of Hare's prescriptivism. First of all, there is the assumption that the value judgments under consideration all imply imperatives; second, there is a peculiar assumption concerning the meanings of "evaluative terms" (these correspond roughly to what I have called "thick ethical concepts"). Before I turn to Sen's way (at this stage in his career) of finding a place for *reasons* in connection with value judgments, I shall now say a word about each of these.

DO VALUE JUDGMENTS IMPLY IMPERATIVES?

One might wonder how value judgments are supposed to stand in *logical relations*, such as *implication*, to anything in that they have no content that is true or false. In the case of statements p and q, which are true or false, to say that p implies q is to say that, if p is true q must be true—indeed (in the case of what is called *logical* implication), there is a logical inference scheme S of which the inference of q from p is an instance, such that *no* instance of S with a true premise has a false conclusion. But if value judgments are not true or false, then "implication" cannot be explained in this way. Hare and Sen are aware of this problem and meet it in different ways. Sen's way is to employ the following test: a value judgment, say, "Capital punishment should be abolished," implies (or "entails") an imperative, say, "Let us abolish capital punishment." Just in case anyone assents to the first and denies the second, then "no sense can be made of the supposition that he did understand what he said, spoke literally, and still meant what he seemed to be saying."[14] But *do* value judgments "entail" imperatives (in this sense of "entails")?

Hare's belief that they do is derived from a belief I criticized in Chapter 3, the belief that value terms are inherently motivational, in the sense that an adjective whose semantic content is that something possesses intrinsic value (or disvalue), is such that anyone who uses it without hypocrisy or insincerity must be *motivated* to approve (or disapprove) of that thing. As Elizabeth Anderson pointed out in a passage I quoted in Chapter 3, "Boredom, weakness, apathy, self-contempt, despair and other motivational states can make a person fail to desire what she judges to be good or desire what she judges to be bad. This prevents the identification of value judgments with expressions of actual desires and preferences, as Hare insists."

If we look at the capital punishment example Sen used, we can see just how implausible this doctrine that "value judgments are ways of assenting to imperatives" actually is. First of all, the imperative, "Let us abolish capital punishment," is a deviant utterance, linguistically speaking, if one is an ordinary citizen, not giving a public speech, and not an influential politician speaking to influential people. The most that an ordinary person could normally say without linguistic oddity would be, "Let us *try* to get capital punishment abolished," or something of that kind. But is it the case that if I say, "Capital punishment should be abolished," and do not assent to "Let us try to get capital punishment abolished," then no sense can be made of the supposition that I understood what I said, spoke literally, and still meant what I seemed to be saying?

Sen himself found reasons to demur from this conclusion

(though not with this example) as I shall discuss. But a simpler reason, and one closely related to Anderson's point, is that I might reply, "I know I should try to get it abolished, but I just don't feel like engaging in politics right now"—or even, "I know I should try, but I guess I am not a very good citizen." The belief that everyone who agrees with the "should be" must at once go along with the imperative, "Let us," is just another form of Hare's unreasonable motivational requirement. And the unreasonable motivational requirement was the very core of "prescriptivism."

"SECONDARILY EVALUATIVE TERMS"

Several examples of what I called "thick ethical concepts" in Part I appear in Sen's "The Nature and Classes of Prescriptive Judgments." Following Hare, Sen says that sometimes such "secondarily evaluative" terms are used "purely descriptively," and sometimes they are used simultaneously to convey a description and to express a "prescription" (an imperative) based upon that description:

> By and large it is the case that value judgments making a significant use of Hare's "secondarily evaluative" terms or expressions are of type J(E) [evaluative judgments], while those confining themselves to the "purely evaluative" terms or expressions can be either J(P) or J(E). When I say, "Your action last Sunday was courageous," not only do I commend it, but I also describe it in a certain way. If instead I say, "Your action was right," I almost certainly commend it, but I *may or may not* mean to imply that it fitted in well with the normally accepted standards of "right" behavior; the same sentence may sometimes stand for a J(P), sometimes for a J(E).[15]

I want to emphasize the way the "secondarily evaluative terms" are interpreted by Sen (who, at this stage, evidently did not wish to recognize the *entanglement* of fact and value that these terms exemplify). I list the two interpretations we have just encountered together with a third (of the adjective "nicer"), which occurs a little later in Sen's paper.[16]

Barbarous = "has certain features usually associated with the notion of barbarity"

Right (when used descriptively) = "fitted in well with the normally accepted standards of 'right' behavior"

Niceness = "may be defined in terms of certain conventional standards, e.g., a 'nicer' girl being one who takes longer to yield to temptations of a certain kind"

It is clear from these three examples that the descriptive meanings of these words are supposed to be captured by what is "usually associated with the notion," or by "normally accepted standards" ("conventional standards"). This is a stupendous mistake—one which, if Sen had not wholly transcended this "prescriptivist" framework, would have made everything he is doing today with his "capabilities" approach to problems of welfare utterly impossible!

It is a mistake in its terms because as a "linguistic analysis" of the meaning of these terms, it implies extremely implausible synonymy relations. For example, if "courageous" were synonymous with, "fits in with normally accepted standards of courageous behavior," then it would be a *contradiction* for someone (Socrates?) to say that the "normally accepted standards" *confuse* courage with rashness. Or to take Sen's own example, if "barbarous" were synonymous with "has certain features usually associated with the notion of barbarity," then to show that capital punishment *isn't* "barbarous," it would suffice to point out that those features that capital punishment has in common with barbarity are not necessary and sufficient for barbarity *as defined by what is "usually associated" with it.*

The problem is that this kind of "analysis" makes a reference to *what most people think when they use the word* a part of the very meaning of a "secondarily evaluative" term. But it is no contradiction to say that many people fail to see that certain acts *aren't* courageous, or that many people fail to see that capital punishment is barbarous, and so on.

A logical positivist would say that when Socrates persuaded us that rash acts do not exemplify courage (if he did succeed in doing this), or when most people in Europe became convinced that capital punishment is barbarous, the *meanings* of the terms "courage" and "barbarous" simply changed. But saying this was part of a larger strategy, in the case of logical positivism, of treating *every* change in the "method of verification" associated with a term as a change in its meaning. This was so obviously just a persuasive redefinition of the term, "meaning," that this very consequence of logical positivism became one of the chief reasons that people gave it up.[17]

But if "courageous" is *not* synonymous with "act that is conventionally *called* 'courageous,'" or something of that kind, and if what it takes to see that we have been misapplying the term is *ethical* insight, then the whole idea that when I describe an act as "courageous" without intending to "commend" it (that is, to endorse a related imperative), I am engaged in "value free description" collapses. "Courageous" may be the precisely apt description of an action without being "value free." This is, of course, just the phenomenon of "entanglement" of fact and value.

REASONS IN ETHICAL DISCUSSION

Earlier in this chapter, I asked the question, "How did Sen find a way to resist the conclusion of the logical positivist A. J. Ayer concerning the relation between a value judgment and its 'reasons'?" The conclusion was that the relation is a merely subjective matter to be studied by psychologists. The importance that Sen attached to being able to do precisely this is evident from his explicit statement of disagreement with the most influential economist of the time, Professor (now Lord) Lionel Robbins, who in his famous treatise on the nature and significance of economics, had written, "it does not seem logically possible to associate the two studies [ethics and economics] in any form but mere juxtaposition. Economics deals with ascertainable facts; ethics with valuation and obligations."[18]

The first step in Sen's procedure was to relax considerably the force of the "imperatives" that are supposed give the (non-descriptive) content of the various value judgments. In Hare's version of prescriptivism, "Capital punishment should be abolished," is equivalent to the imperative, "Let us abolish capital punishment," where this means: *"No matter what reasons may be given against doing it,* let us abolish capital punishment." A value judgment that is equivalent to an absolutely unconditional imperative of this sort is called a "compulsive" judgment by Sen, and Sen's first point is that a great many, perhaps the large majority, of all value judgments are non-compulsive: "There is another kind of judgment, such that a judgment of this kind in favour of X against Y *implies* an imperative in favour of X in a choice between the two, *if* one denies at the same time all conceivable value judgments giving a reason in favour of choosing Y against X."[19] Sen gives the following example of a familiar kind of value judgment that is "non-compulsive": if someone says that something is "nicer" than something else, this does not imply that they endorse the imperative, "Let us choose it." All kinds of reasons might override the greater "niceness": it might cost too much, or it might be out of fashion, and so on. Note that Sen has rejected Hare's thesis that every value judgment just *is* a way of endorsing a *particular* imperative.

What I find more important, however, is Sen's discussion of a different—and very familiar—distinction, the distinction between "basic" and "non-basic" value judgments:

> There is another useful method of classifying value judgments which we may now discuss. A value judgment can be called "basic" to a person if no conceivable revision of factual assumptions can make him revise the judgment. If such revisions can take place, the judgment is "non-basic" in his value system. [Note that "non-basic" is not the same as "non-compulsive." Non-compulsiveness has to do with the defeasibility of the relation between the value judgment and the imperative to choose the positively valued item—or not to choose the negatively valued item—while non-basicness has to do

with the revisability of the value judgment itself.] For example, a person may express the judgment, "A rise in national income measured at base year prices indicates a better economic situation." We may ask him whether he will stick to this judgment under all factual circumstances, and go on inquiring, "Would you say the same if the circumstances were such and such (e.g., the poor were poorer and the rich a lot richer)?" If it turns out that he will revise the judgment under certain factual circumstances, then the judgment can be taken to be non-basic in his value system. If, on the other hand, there is no factual situation when a certain person will regard killing a human being to be justifiable, then not killing a human being is a basic value judgment in his system.[20]

Ayer had argued that there cannot be either a "logical sense" or a "scientific sense" in which "reasons" can support a value judgment.[21] Sen calls Ayer's presentation "misleading," and writes, "Someone disputing a value judgment put forward by someone else can have a scientific discussion on the validity of the value judgment by examining the scientific truth of the underlying factual premises."[22] And he continues:

Now, if the judgment expressed happened to be a "basic" one in the value system of the person expressing it, then and only then could it be claimed that there can be no factual method of disputing the judgment. That all value judgments are not basic is easy to show in practically anyone's value system. If someone entertained only basic value judgments and no others, he would be able to answer every moral question that he can answer without knowing any of the facts; but such people seem to be, to say the least, rare.

. . . Consider, for example, the value judgment, "The government should not raise the money supply more than in proportion to the national output," based on a factual theory relating money supply and output to inflation. If this theory is disputed, which is a legitimate reason against the value judgment in question, the person may move on to a more fundamental value judgment, "The government should not do anything that leads to inflation." If that too is based on some factual assumption, making it non-basic, the process of moving backwards, as it were, may be repeated. . . . In this way one might hope to reach ultimately in this person's value system some basic value judgments.[23]

Up to this point, Sen has refuted Ayer (who writes as if all value judgments were "basic," just as Hare writes as if all value judgments were "compulsive"), but he has not said anything that a greater logical positivist than Ayer could not accept. Hans Reichenbach, for example, distinguished between imperatives and *entailed* imperatives, and argued in a similar way that rational discussion of the entailments of one's basic imperatives is possible.[24] But Sen goes much further. Without ever quite saying that the whole doctrine that there must *be* "basic value judgments" in any rational value system is wrong (as John Dewey did throughout his philosophical career), he in effect argues that it is *unverifiable* that any value judgment is basic![25]

Sen's clearest statement on this point occurs when he quarrels with Lionel Robbins. Robbins had written:

If we disagree about ends it is a case of thy blood or mine—or live or let live according to the importance of the difference, or the relative strength of our opponents. But if we disagree about means, then scientific analysis can often help us resolve our differences. If we disagree about the morality of the taking of interest (and we understand what we are talking about), then there is no room for argument.[26]

Sen's comment is:

The crucial difficulty with this approach is that it is not quite clearly determinable whether a certain end, or the corresponding value judgment stating the end, is basic or not. To take Robbins' own example, how can one be so certain that a difference on the morality of taking interest must be of a *basic* kind, i.e., why must both parties' judgments on the morality of taking interest be necessarily basic? The assumption that judgments on certain specific fields (e.g., the rightness of taking interest) must be basic in everyone's value system, does not seem to be particularly realistic.[27]

Sen then considers the possibility of a "test of basicness." *Asking* the person concerned naturally occurs as a possibility. "But since no one would have had occasion to consider all conceivable alternative factual circumstances and to decide whether in any of the cases he would change the judgment or not, his answer to the question may not be conclusive." Another test is to ask the person to consider hypothetical and even counterfactual revisions of factual assumptions, but "this process never establishes basicness, though it can establish that the judgment is not non-basic in any obviously relevant way." Sen concludes, "It is interesting to note that some value judgments are demonstrably non-basic, but no value judgment is demonstrably basic."[28]

To show that all this is no idle logical exercise, Sen then considers utilitarianism in detail and shows that in their compulsive forms, the various better-known versions of utilitarianism are best construed as *non-basic*.[29] The moral is clear: when we are dealing with any important value disagreement, we assume that facts are irrelevant at our peril. No convincing logical reason can be given for the *logical* irrelevance of fact to value judgments, even if we accept the positivist conception of what a "fact" is.

5 ON THE RATIONALITY OF PREFERENCES

SOME YEARS AGO I published a paper contesting the legitimacy of the completeness axiom of standard decision theory and read the paper to various groups, including groups of economists.[1] One of the objections I encountered was so startling that I decided to share it and explore the issues it opens up—issues about no less a matter than the rationality of existential choices.[2] But first I need to review my original argument.

RATIONAL PREFERENCE THEORY

Although certain theorists[3] have found ways in the last twenty years or so of dropping some of the very strong axioms about preference adopted by von Neumann and Morgenstern, the "classical" results von Neumann and Morgenstern obtained depend crucially on those assumptions.[4] Without them, it is not possible, for example,

to prove the celebrated theorem that any *rational* system of preferences can be represented by a "utility scale," a function that assigns
real numbers to maximal "commodity bundles" in such a way that
a commodity bundle A is preferred to a commodity bundle B, or B
is preferred to A, or the agent doesn't care which she gets (is "indifferent"), as the "utility" of A is greater than, less than, or equal to
the "utility" of B. Preference orderings in which there are no in-
comparabilities are said to be *complete;* thus this theorem implies
that all truly rational agents have complete preference orderings.[5]

From the time this theorem was articulated, there were those
who found both the axioms and the theorem in question counterin-
tuitive, and one of the issues around which argument has long
swirled is whether it is not possible for a perfectly rational being to
regard certain goods as *incomparable.*[6] If we symbolize the statement that a "commodity bundle" (which may be a whole way of
life) x is at least as highly ranked as a "commodity bundle" (or way
of life) y, as xRy, and the statement that I am "indifferent" as "xRy &
yRx," then for two ways of life x and y to be incomparable, given
my state of mind (my "preference ordering") is just for neither of
the two alternatives: xRy and yRx to obtain. The traditional view
(the view of von Neumann and Morgenstern) was that this is impossible, that is, it postulated that:

(1) $(x)(y) (xRy \lor yRx)$[7]

But was this reasonable?

In the paper I mentioned at the beginning of the chapter, I argued that it is not. As an example, consider the following: suppose
an agent, call her "Theresa," is torn (just as Pascal imagined in his
famous wager) between an ascetic religious way of life and a sensual one. Theresa may know that if she were to choose the sensual
way of life, she would prefer to have as a lover A, who seems to her
to be more attractive and responsive, to the slightly plainer and less
responsive suitor B. Call these choices x and y, and let z be the as-

cetic religious life. As long as Theresa regards the two ways of life as each being worth considering but "incomparable," then (in her "ordering") ~xRz & ~zRx and also ~yRz & ~zRy, which is in violation of (1).[8]

Those who, like myself, wish to defend Theresa from the charge of "irrationality" will, of course, point out that the intuitive meaning of "indifference" is that the agent doesn't care which she gets, and that although, in Theresa's case, it is true that ~xRz & ~zRx, it is not that Theresa doesn't care in the sense that she is willing to let a coin-toss decide, for example; it is that *she has not decided,* and there seems to be all the difference in the world between these two cases.[9] Denying the very possibility of a difference between alternatives that the agent regards as perfectly substitutable and alternatives that the agent regards as presenting her with an existential decision, looks "fishy."[10] And it ought to look fishy, I would argue, for there is no good ground for regarding Theresa as "irrational."

What makes her "irrational" (if we assume the traditional axioms) isn't that her preferences lack transitivity; she is not a person who violates (or claims to violate) the principle that

(2) $(x)(y)(z)[(xRy \ \& \ yRz) \rightarrow xRz]$

but she does violate a principle that probably those who have not studied decision theory would never have even considered as a possible assumption for "rational preference theory," namely, the principle that *the negation of the weak preference relation* (R) *is transitive.*[11] It is indeed the case that she violates this principle, for if we let x and y be the two sorts of lovers and z be the ascetic religious life, we have stipulated that ~xRz and also ~zRy, so the principle in question, namely:

(3) $(x)(y)(z)[(\sim xRz \ \& \ \sim zRy) \rightarrow \sim xRy]$

requires that to be "rational" Theresa must not rank x at least as high as y.[12] Since the supposed distinction between "incomparabil-ity" and mere "indifference" turns on such cases—cases that violate the transitivity of "is not weakly preferred"—the distinction is inap-plicable to agents who are truly rational. Poor Theresa is irrational.

But why should we accept (3)? The difficulty that threatens us if we violate this axiom is easy to describe. Suppose I prefer x to y, and I claim that a third "commodity" z is such that $\sim xRz$ & $\sim zRx$ and also such that $\sim yRz$ & $\sim zRy$. Then a decision theorist can, it seems, embarrass me with the following argument: "Suppose," she says, "I were to offer you a choice between x and y. Since you prefer x to y, you would choose x. But suppose you are confronted with the al-ternatives x and z. Since you have no preference, you cannot com-plain if instead of offering you a choice, I simply give you z rather than x. If you complain, that will show that you did prefer x to z, contrary to your statement that $\sim xRz$ & $\sim zRx$. Isn't that right?"

If I agree that it is, the decision theorist will continue, "But now, having gotten you to agree that it's all right if I give you z, I can say, 'Since you say that you have no preference as between z and y, and it has turned out to be inconvenient to give you z after all, I will give you y instead.' If you complain at this stage, that will show that you did prefer y to z, contrary to your statement that $\sim yRz$ & $\sim zRy$. But if you don't complain, then in two steps I will have moved you—with your consent at each step—from receiving x to receiving y, that is from a preferred to a less preferred alternative."[13]

In reply to this argument, I suggested that it is part of choices like Theresa's that the alternatives include, as an essential part of what is being evaluated, that they be selected by the agent herself, of her own free will, and not decided for her by the decision theo-rist (or by a bureaucrat, or a psychologist, or by a flip of a coin . . .).[14] The decision theorist's argument that if Theresa has indeed not yet formed a preference, she cannot rationally object to being *given* z rather than x—that any objection on her part will "show" that she really does already prefer x to z, contrary to her expressed state-ment that $\sim xRz$ & $\sim zRx$—is quite wrong. Theresa *can* rationally object, not on the ground that she would have preferred to have been "given" x rather than z, but on the ground that "giving" her either is giving her neither of the options that interest her. What she wants is—after reflection—a sensual life chosen of her own free will (and if that turns out to be the choice, then if possible A rather than B) *or* an ascetic religious life chosen of her own free will, and saying to her either, "we will choose for you that you shall have a sensual life (and A as a lover)," or, "we will choose for you that you shall have an ascetic religious life," is giving her nothing that she can value at all. Reading ~xRz & ~zRx as, "the agent is indifferent as between x and z" (or alternatively as, "x is no worse than z and z is no worse than x, from the agent's point of view"), simply assumes that all choices may be regarded as choices between mere "commodities," that is, between goods whose value to the agent does not depend on whether she herself chooses them, or whether they just "come" to her (by chance, as it might be). But if someone "decides" to give Theresa one way of life or the other on the ground that she does not (yet) have a preference for one over the other, he deprives her of precisely what is most important to her, namely that the decision shall be her own. Thinking of everything as a "commodity" will necessarily blind one to the most elementary facts about the moral life.

IS CONCERN FOR AUTONOMY REALLY RATIONAL?

As I mentioned at the outset, I have presented the preceding arguments to various audiences, including audiences of political scientists and economists as well as philosophers, and one of the responses I received (from an economist) occasioned this chapter. That response was to the effect that the concern for her autonomy that I ascribed to Theresa, the importance that she attaches to the decision's being her own, is itself irrational.

The argument offered in support of this surprising claim was not without a certain ingenuity. My interlocutor argued that there are two possibilities in a case like Theresa's. Either something internal to Theresa's makeup already determines what the outcome of her soul-searching is going to be, or the outcome is objectively indeterminate, as far as the "internal" variables are concerned. In the first case, we can say that her rational preference function already determines Theresa's decision; it is just that she is not aware of it. Her claim that there is no fixed R-relation between x and z and between y and z is the product of ignorance; from a God's-eye view it is false. What of the second case?

In the second case, since the internal factors do not determine what Theresa will decide, it will be external variables—probably ones of which Theresa is not even conscious, and which may be quite accidental—that will cause the decision to go one way or the other. But to feel strongly about whether it is the decision theorist or a bunch of nameless environmental factors that cause one's decision is to have a feeling with no rational basis! Autonomy is bunk.

To be sure, I doubt that the economics profession could really adopt this line of argument as its official reply to the objection that I raised. For one thing, rational preference theory is supposed to be "value neutral," and the whole point of this objection is to show that a particular value, the value Theresa assigns to this decision's being her own, is "irrational."[15] Moreover, the idea that anything that is present inside me that will eventually cause me to choose one way or another is to be described as an already existent "preference" is highly problematic.[16] But let us set these difficulties aside; the question that interests me is the challenge posed by my interlocutor to the rationality of valuing autonomy.

Discussing that challenge could easily lead us into deep waters. I am not myself a "compatibilist" about free will, but *those* waters are too deep for wading, so here I shall confine myself to what even Humeans can accept: even if it should be the case that all our actions are causally determined far in advance, we can still meaningfully distinguish between what, in an everyday sense of the expression, we "do of our own free will" and what we merely suffer or undergo.[17] In addition, I take it that even if one adopts the David-sonian view that reasons are (a species of) causes, no one supposes that *all* the causes of our decisions are reasons.

These (elementary) philosophical distinctions are enough to give a preliminary response to the challenge. (Since I don't recall my interlocutor's name, I shall refer to him simply as the Challenger.) Part of what is important to Theresa is that her action be taken "of her own free will," at least in the everyday sense. But the Challenger can grant that much without abandoning his argument. "If what she objects to is the decision theorist's making the decision," he might say, "she could flip a coin instead. If she were willing to flip a coin, rather than wait for what you call an 'existential decision' to form itself within her soul, presumably she would agree that she was 'indifferent' in my sense of 'indifferent'; so the question is, what rational reason does she have to let a bunch of nameless environmental factors determine what her so-called existential decision will be, when she could just flip a coin? She could, after all, take satisfaction in the idea that flipping the coin and deciding to abide by the result was something she did 'of her own free will,' if *that's* the relevant value."

So to the requirement (imposed by Theresa herself) that whatever she decides to do must be of her own free will, we must add a further stipulation: Theresa must be able to give satisfactory reasons for her decision—not metaphysical reasons, but just the sort of reasons that actually have weight in human lives. It is not relevant to Theresa what the merely causal determinants of her action will be, but it is relevant (relevant to her) what *reasons* she will, in the end, be able to give.

In order to improve our purchase on this issue, let us change the example from a decision for or against a particular sort of religious life to a secular decision. Let us suppose that Theresa decides, in the end, against both hedonism and asceticism and, after a certain lapse of time, finds herself choosing a career. She is a physician, and she has narrowed the choice to becoming a wealthy specialist versus practicing medicine in a very poor community in India. (Perhaps it *is* the original choice in a different guise!) She feels the attraction of both but also finds the choice hard because the sorts of life she will have are so different. Once again she has not made the decision, "who to be." But the idea of just "flipping a coin" is utterly repellant. Is this irrational?[18]

Notice that, mere "causes" aside, the reasons she will offer if she chooses the more bourgeois path are very different from the reasons she will offer if she chooses the path of courageous social service. If she chooses the bourgeois path, she will very likely say that the hardships and risks of the other life were just too great, and that she "owes it to herself" to have the material rewards she would have to pass up to go into the life in the village in India. If she chooses the second path, she will say that it gives meaning to her life and that it enables her to be a healer in the highest sense of the term, which is what doctors are, after all, supposed to be.

There are different levels of philosophical depth at which the Challenger might choose to respond to these points. He may choose to regard all such reasons as mere "rationalizations." But more simply, he may point out that while it may be a value to have reasons to offer for one's decisions, his original argument is one he can repeat at the level of the reasons. Either the reasons Theresa will offer in the end (including so-called higher order reasons) are already in place, or they are not. . . . And so on. In the next section, I explore this dialectic further.

IS IT RATIONAL TO WANT REASONS?

Let us now see what happens when I try to repeat the Challenger's argument at the level of Theresa's future reasons. It is of course true that the Challenger can do this, but isn't there something more than a little paradoxical about questioning whether it is rational to want to be able to give reasons for one's actions? But once again, let us try to dig a little deeper.

For this purpose, let me actually spell out the Challenger's argument as it would look if applied at the level of reasons. Once again, I shall set aside the case in which the reasons that Theresa will eventually give for whatever decision she makes were already present in her soul (whether she knew it or not) and in which her final decision is simply the culmination of a process of reflection leading to the attainment of increased self-knowledge to the discovery of what her true preference ordering had been all along. I shall stipulate that, from the point of view of an Omniscient Psychologist, the outcome of the process of soul-searching and decision-making that Theresa engaged in had an outcome that was genuinely indeterminate (at the time at which she might have described the ways of life in question as representing what were for her, at that moment, genuinely incomparable values). If she later offers reasons for the action, even higher-level reasons for considering one kind of reason to be more important to her (or even intrinsically more important) than another sort of reason, I shall suppose that if she had made the decision the other way, she would have had some suitable conflicting set of different higher-order reasons to give for that other choice. I shall also suppose that at the time her state of mind could be represented by the statement that the two ways of life are incomparable (or by a set of statements violating the transitivity of the negation of the relation "R" like the ones we considered earlier) it was indeterminate which set of higher-order reasons she would eventually opt for.[19] As Wittgenstein reminds us, reasons have to come to an end somewhere. What we are imagining to be objectively indeterminate is where Theresa's reasons will come to an end.

At this point, as I anticipated with my remark about the paradoxical nature of the question, the Challenger's argument will hit a snag. To continue arguing at the level of reasons as he did at the level of decisions, the Challenger would have to say something like the following: "In the end, Theresa's choice of reasons, just like her choice of a way of life, is going to be determined by a bunch of nameless environmental factors, and why is it rational for Theresa to let a bunch of nameless environmental factors determine which reasons she will accept as binding when she could just flip a coin?" But the argument falters, for one cannot simply choose to acknowledge the force of a reason. I can decide to flip a coin, and to go to the movies if the toss comes up heads and to continue working on my lecture for tomorrow morning if it comes up tails, but I cannot decide to (sincerely) accept the argument that I will stay home and work on my lecture because it is irresponsible to come to my own class unprepared or that I will (sincerely) acknowledge the force of the argument that, although in general it is irresponsible to come to my class unprepared, at this point my need for recreation is overriding, depending on which way the coin falls. And if I do not sincerely accept R as the better reason for acting, then I cannot act *for the reason* R. If the desire to act from reasons whose binding force is sincerely acknowledged by herself is itself a legitimate value for Theresa, then Theresa has an excellent reason (relative to her "preferences") for rejecting the suggestion that she simply flip a coin. For if she were to simply flip a coin, she would end up choosing whichever way of life the coin toss pointed to on grounds other than the possession of *reasons for that way of life that appear to her to be valid*. Once again, we can argue that it is internal to the action that she wants to take that, no matter which of the alternatives it may be, it should include the possession of reasons that should be seen from within that very life as having force, and that constitute the way of life as the way of life it is. Indeed, it may not be possible for anyone to live either the life of a busy and successful doctor in the United States or the life of a doctor to the poor in an Indian village simply on the basis of a coin toss; both lives involve stress, and the life of a doctor in a remote village involves hardship as well. It may be that without the possession of a whole internal value system, including the possession of reasons, one would not have the strength to go through with either way.

INTERNAL AND EXTERNAL REASONS

At this point, I cannot help remarking that the skepticism as to the rationality of insisting that the agent herself be allowed to make her existential choices (and that she be able to give reasons for them, even if the reasons are not available to the agent prior to the existential choice itself)[20] that I attributed to my Challenger bears a certain evocative resemblance—at least I find it evocative—to Bernard Williams's well-known skepticism about "external reasons."[21] This is not just free association on my part. What bothers the Challenger is that in the cases we have been considering, the agent lacks what Williams calls an "internal reason" to choose one way of life or the other, or at least she does not *yet* have an internal reason to choose one way of life or the other. Like Bernard Williams, the Challenger feels that talk of "external reasons," reasons that are good reasons for the agent even though the agent does not acknowledge them as such because they are not part of the agent's "motivational set," is "false or incoherent."[22] So it seems to him that Theresa is simply *without reason* to decide one way or the other, and hence he does not see why she is unwilling to let someone else make the decision for her, or to let a coin toss decide. I do not mean to suggest that Bernard Williams would follow the Challenger in this; I am sure that he would not. What I want to think about is how he might justify refusing to follow the Challenger's line of argument.

Of course, Bernard Williams could reject the Challenger's argument on just the grounds that I gave. To describe something as a choice between two ways of life is to say that part of what one wants is to find reasons and not just deeds, reasons that one can make one's own, and that will come to have a binding force in one's life. And reasons are not the sort of thing that someone else can choose or that can be left up to the toss of a coin. But if the Challenger is sophisticated (or Mephistophelian?) enough, he will make the following response: "How does someone talk who does this thing that you call acknowledging 'the force of reasons'? Perhaps they talk the language of objective duty ('I saw where my duty lay'), or they talk the language of self-discovery ('I discovered what my deepest needs were,' or 'I discovered what the most satisfying life for me would be'). But the former sort of talk is a blatant appeal to external reasons, and the latter sort, if it isn't a claim to have discovered something that was already in my motivational set, is simply a disguised appeal to external reasons.[23] So if we really have a need for that sort of talk, which may sadly be the case, it is a need for an irrational belief, a belief that external reasons can have something mysterious called 'force.' And isn't it time that we outgrew that need?"

What ought to trouble Bernard Williams about this rhetorical question is the fact that talk of external reasons is not simply metaphysical talk, it is ethical talk, talk that we engage in from within the ethical life itself. People of good will regularly include in their descriptions of their "values" or "preferences" or "desires" a value or preference or desire *to do what is right*. To be a person of good will is precisely to care about *doing the right thing*. When I am in doubt as to what to do, I frequently ask myself what the right thing to do is, and I justify doing one thing or the other at the end (or very often do) by saying that I realized that I ought to do so and so. Similar remarks apply when the kind of rightness at stake is not moral rightness in the narrow sense, but rightness from the standpoint of what would be the good in my life, what would be the best life for me. Now, as Peter Strawson reminded in a very early paper, talk of knowing what the right thing to do is, does not have to be metaphysical talk; that sort of talk is internal to ethical life itself.[24] When Williams tells us that talk of external reasons is "false or incoherent," he seems—intentionally or unintentionally—to be adopting a profoundly revisionist stance towards our actual moral life, and it is this that I just imagined my Challenger (or his Mephistophelian counterpart) exposing. The difficulty would be a difficulty for Williams even if he were not a cognitivist in ethics because noncognitivists in ethics (for example, "quasirealists" such as Simon Blackburn or old-fashioned emotivists such as Charles Stevenson) regularly claim that the adoption of their noncognitivism as an answer to the question of the status of value judgments does not have any implications one way or the other for first-order ethical talk. They claim that first-order ethical talk can go on just as it does even if one regards all ethical sentences as expressions of attitude, disguised imperatives, or something of that kind. But if to dismiss talk of external reasons as "false or incoherent" isn't to dismiss talk of *knowing, discovering, realizing,* and indeed talk of *truth* in ethics, then it is hard to see what is being recommended.[25]

Moreover, Bernard Williams is not a noncognitivist. He claims that in the ordinary sense of "true" and "false," ethical judgments can be true and false. I will be reminded, however, that Williams draws a sharp (in my view, *too* sharp) distinction between "thick" and "thin" ethical concepts.[26] Perhaps it is only with respect to the thin ethical concepts such as "right" that Williams would say that talk of discovering, knowing, and the like is mere "bluff."[27] With respect to thick ethical concepts, on Williams's view, the situation is different. One can *know* (provided one is within the appropriate "social world") that an act is "cruel" or "loving" or "stupid" or "silly," and so on. If finding out that an act is cruel or loving or silly is simply finding out that that is what my cultural peers call it, then Williams would seem to be committed to the same sharp distinction between speaking "within a language game" and "speaking outside of language games" that Rorty draws.[28] That dichotomy seems to me to be wholly untenable. In any case, if the truth-valuedness of ethical language comes down to no more (on Williams's view) than what Rorty would regard as objectivity from within a language game, it amounts to no more than consensus in a particular culture.

If Williams misses the seriousness of his own skepticism with respect to external reasons, the reason is to be found in the way that he poses the issue. When Williams does imagine someone who is not moved by a consideration involving a thick ethical concept, his case is of a person (Owen Wingrave) who simply rejects the consideration in question; the value in question is simply not his. But there is a different sort of case that he might have considered. Imagine someone who is criticized "externally" for behaving *selfishly.* Such a person will not, as a rule, simply reject unselfishness as a value. And we cannot say that criticizing him (rightly or wrongly) for behaving selfishly is making a charge that is "false or incoherent." The effect of Williams's choice of examples is to focus attention exclusively on the question whether lacking certain values—or even lacking a good will completely—is a form of *irrationality*.[29] But the terms "rational" and "irrational" have been used so often as footballs in intellectual debates in the last two centuries (including debates in decision theory), that that question may well be an empty one. The question I have tried to raise here requires a different sort of example. Suppose we are dealing with someone who has a good will, someone who certainly does not want to perform an action if that action is, say, a selfish one, but who simply does not agree with other people that the action would be a selfish one. Suppose, further, that the person in question has no "internal reason" to accept the view that the action *is* "selfish."[30] Then there will be a gulf between the ethical perspective on the moral disagreement in question and Bernard Williams's metaphysical perspective. From the ethical perspective—which is the perspective of the agent himself—the claim that the action in question is a selfish one would, if it were true, count as a reason against performing the action, and the reason the agent is not moved is not that external reasons are not coherent reasons or anything of that kind, but simply that the agent does not agree that the action is selfish. From Williams's metaphysical perspective, it would seem that saying that the agent is wrong because he is mistaken about the action's not being a selfish one (in a case when there is no consensus in the relevant "social world") is just a form of high-minded rhetoric, just another way of packaging an appeal to external reasons, to reasons that are (according to Williams) "false or incoherent." In short, once one has accepted that existence of a gulf between internal and external reasons, and the doctrine that appeals to external reasons are "false or incoherent," it is difficult to see how one can stop short of a Rortian relativism with respect to ethics.

CONCLUSION

If all I had wanted to do was rebut my Challenger (and not discuss Bernard Williams at all), I had a much quicker route available to me than the circuitous path I have traversed. I could, after all, have contented myself with pointing out that one cannot reject an end as "irrational" unless one already assumes that there are rational and irrational ends. Moreover, in speaking of Theresa's desire to "make up her own mind" as an *irrational* end, the Challenger was appealing to no value in Theresa's "motivational set"; he was assuming his own values and treating them as ones that Theresa was unreasonable to reject. In short, he has to reject Williams's view on the "falsity or incoherence" of external reasons to make his argument at all; that means that he cannot appeal to it at a later stage in his argument, as I just imagined him to do.

So why did I want to talk about Williams? I brought Williams into the picture because, in a much more sophisticated way, he is worried about what the Challenger was worried about. Like the Challenger, Williams cannot see how a decision can be rational if it is left undetermined by all the elements in what he refers to as the agent's "motivational set." Of course, he does not make the dumb mistake that my Challenger made, the mistake of arguing that if Theresa's decision cannot be called "rational," then it must be irrational. Certainly he would advise all of us—including Theresa herself—to refrain from speaking of such decisions as either "rational" or "irrational." And, as I pointed out, it makes things much easier for such a view if we allow ourselves to imagine that whatever reason Theresa will eventually give as the grounds for her decision (say, for example, that she went to India, or joined *Médecins sans Frontières*, or whatever, because she wanted to make a significant contribution, and this was the best way to do that) was one that she would have rejected out of hand before because it was not yet in her "motivational set." But this talk of "motivational sets" (and of things being in and out of motivational sets) as if these were hard natural scientific facts entirely obscures the issue. In real life, Theresa may well have described her problem at the outset as "wanting to make the greatest contribution with her life," and she may now describe what happened by saying that she "came to see" that this was the way to do that. If we think that speaking of rational connections as things we can be right or wrong about is simply mystery-mongering, then this will be rejected as, at best, rhetoric. But Theresa is not doing *metaphysics;* she is living her life with the aid of an ethical standpoint. The language of *coming to see* what that standpoint requires of one is internal to that standpoint and not a piece of transcendental machinery that is required to provide a foundation for it. If it is possible to do science without supposing that one needs a metaphysical foundation for the enterprise, it is equally possible to live an ethical life without supposing that one needs a metaphysical foundation. (Nor must we accept an emotivist or "antirealist" or "quasirealist" metaphysical story according to which the claims we make when we occupy the particular ethical standpoint we do are not "really" true and coherent; that sort of story is just another epicycle in the trajectory from absurd realism to absurd antirealism and back again.)[31] As John Dewey urged long ago, the objectivity that ethical claims require is not the kind that is provided by a Platonic or other foundation that is there in advance of our engaging in ethical life and ethical reflection; it is the ability to withstand the sort of criticism that arises in the problematic situations that we actually encounter, the kind of criticism for which, as John McDowell remarks, "the appropriate image is Neurath's, in which a sailor overhauls his ship while it is afloat."[32]

What Williams and my naive Challenger have in common is the belief that talk of reasons for one to choose x must be either reconstrued as talk of internal causes (in a sense of "cause" in which internal causes are hard natural facts) or else rejected as talk of suspect metaphysical items. But just as talk of following a rule is not reducible to talk of physical causes for one's observed behavior, and yet is not on that account to be rejected as talk of such suspect metaphysical items as invisible rails guiding the mind, so talk of reasons for one to do so-and-so is not reducible to talk of causes for one's observed behavior, and yet is not on that account to be rejected as talk of such suspect metaphysical items as Platonic Forms or Transcendental Egos.[33] Ethical talk needs no metaphysical story to support it (or, in a postmodernist version of the metaphysical temptation, to "deconstruct" it); it only needs what ethical talk—both in the narrower senses of "ethical," and in the wide sense of talk about the good life—has always needed: good will, intelligence, and respect for what can be seen as grounds and difficulties from within the ethical standpoint itself.[34]

6 ARE VALUES MADE OR DISCOVERED?

I BELIEVE THAT, in a certain way, the first modern philosopher to raise the question as to whether values—both legal and
moral values—are "made or discovered" was Hobbes. Hobbes's
view was that moral values and legal values are of essentially the
same kind and that moral judgments and legal judgments alike become intersubjectively valid when they are declared to be so by
"the sovereign." In Hobbes's view, there is little point to distinguishing between moral and legal validity, and Hobbes, in fact, does not
usually so distinguish. (Indeed, in Hobbes's view, even cases of
vagueness [of words], when they result in contention, are to be resolved in the same way, by an appropriate stipulation of "the sovereign"—who, I should add, need not be a king; a legislature may
also be the sovereign, in Hobbes's theory.) One might say that
Hobbes was not only a legal positivist, but also an unusual kind of
moral positivist.[1]

While Hobbes's position with respect to legal validity continues to have its defenders, his conception of moral validity does not; no one today defends the view that (moral) right and wrong are whatever the sovereign says they are. For that reason, questions about moral validity and legal validity now have to be distinguished, even if at the end we face the question as to the exact relation between them.

A DEWEYAN VIEW OF VALUATION

My own answer to the question, "Are values made or discovered," is the one that I believe John Dewey would have given, namely that we make ways of dealing with problematical situations and we discover which ones are better and which worse. Obviously a good deal has to be said about what this means and why and how it is responsive to the question.

It will seem unresponsive to the question if one supposes that the judgment that one way of solving a problem is better than another must always be a purely "instrumental" judgment in the classical sense, that is, must be no more than a judgment to the effect that putative solution A is more efficient than proposed solution B with respect to values and goals already assumed (with respect to what Dewey calls "ends in view"). But this is not the way that Dewey sees matters. For him "inquiry" in the widest sense, that is human dealings with problematical situations, involves incessant reconsideration of both means *and* ends; it is not the case that each person's goals are cast in concrete in the form of a "rational preference function" that is somehow mysteriously imbedded in his or her individual mind, or that all we are allowed to do as long as we are "rational" is look for more efficient means to these immutable but idiosyncratic goals or values. Any inquiry has both "factual" presuppositions, including presuppositions as to the efficiency of various means to various ends, and "value" presuppositions, and if resolving our problem is difficult, then we may well want to reconsider both our "factual" assumptions and our goals. In short, changing one's values is not only a legitimate way of solving a problem, but frequently the only way of solving a problem.[2]

The claim has, of course, been advanced that what seems phenomenologically to be a decision to change one's values is "really" only a case of discovering new means to some still more fundamental (and higher-ranked) values that were "there" all along; this is not only armchair psychology, but (the worst form of armchair psychology), a priori psychology.[3]

Dewey, then, is not just talking about finding better means to preexisting ends-in-view (about what Habermas calls "means-ends rationality," *Zweckmittelrationalität,* or about what Kant called "hypothetical imperatives"). Dewey is really talking about learning through experimentation and discussion how to increase the amount of *good* in our lives. Once we see that this is what Dewey means and that he is serious about this, then very different objections arise.

Those objections can be divided into two classes. Objections of one kind I will call "Rortian objections," and I will consider those objections immediately; objections of the other kind I will call "reductionist objections," and I will consider them in a few minutes.

RORTY AND DEWEY

Readers of Rorty are well aware that Dewey is one of his heroes. Rorty hails Dewey's rejection of any supposedly fundamental fact/value dichotomy, either ontological or epistemological, and he thoroughly agrees with Dewey that serious inquiry in difficult situations results as often in a revision or redefinition of our "values" as in an improvement of our "factual knowledge."[4] Yet Ralph Sleeper's accurate description of what he calls Dewey's "objective realism," while it contains much that Rorty would agree with, points to a side of Dewey that Rorty regards as lamentably metaphysical. Sleeper writes:

Objects of knowledge, he [Dewey] wants to show, may be instrumental to satisfaction, but their warrant does not consist in that instrumentality. Dewey takes great pains to demonstrate that "warranted assertions" are the reliable means of obtaining desired results, that they function in controlled activity designed to resolve problematical situations and produce valued consequences. But he also takes pains to demonstrate that those valued consequences are reliable only when the means employed to obtain them are causally related to objective reality. He wants to show not merely that matters of fact *have* value as instrumental to satisfaction, but that they *are* values. He wants to demonstrate not only that there is no conceptually valid basis for the distinction between factual judgment and value judgment, but that there is no basis for an ontological distinction either. He seeks to attain by means of an objective realism and a logic of scientific method what James despaired of achieving except by the method of tenacity, and what Peirce thought could be reached only through objective idealism.[5]

What Rorty would disagree with (not in Sleeper's account of Dewey's position, but in the position itself) are the references to "objective reality"—what Sleeper calls Dewey's "objective realism." Again and again, Rorty argues that the notion of "objective reality" is empty since we cannot stand outside of our skins and compare our notions with (supposed) objective reality as it is "in itself."[6]

The idea of reality as it is "in itself," that is, as we would describe it if we knew the terms that describe its *intrinsic* nature, is apparently the only possible meaning that Rorty sees for the notion of "objective reality." If the metaphysical sort of realism that posits "things in themselves" with an "intrinsic nature" makes no sense, then Rorty supposes, neither does the notion of objectivity. We should drop all talk of objectivity and talk of "solidarity" instead.[7] The solutions or resolutions we find to our problematical situations are at best solutions or resolutions by the standards of our culture (which Rorty takes to be liberal, democratic, Whiggish, and European) and not by some supposed further standard or standards of "objectivity."

There is something I find very strange about this reaction of

Rorty's.[8] Although I join Rorty in rejecting certain traditional meta-physical notions, I do not believe that giving up these notions (finding them, in the end, quite empty) requires us to draw the conclusions that he does. What I agree with is that the idea of comparing my thoughts and beliefs, on the one hand, with things "as they are in themselves," on the other, makes no sense; but I do not agree that this idea is a necessary presupposition of the everyday thought that there are objects that are not parts of thought or language, or of the equally everyday thought that what we say about those objects sometimes *gets the facts right.* Perhaps I can bring out what I find unsatisfying about the conclusion Rorty draws by means of an analogy. Even though I cannot stand outside my own skin and compare the future as it will be after my death with my thoughts and ideas about that future, I do not for that reason stop supposing that there are events that will happen after I die, and I take out life insurance in order to affect the course of those events. Or, to take another example, even though I would agree with Rorty that I cannot step outside of my own skin and compare my friends' experiences "as they are in themselves" with my thoughts and ideas about them, I continue to sympathize with my friends and share their joys and worry about their troubles. I agree with Rorty that the metaphysical assumption that there is a fundamental di-chotomy between "intrinsic" properties of things and "relational" properties of things makes no sense; but that does not lead me to view the thoughts and experiences of my friends as *just* the intentional objects of beliefs that help me "cope." If I did, what sense would it make to talk of "solidarity"? The very notion of solidarity requires commonsense realism about the objective existence of the people one is in "solidarity" with. What these examples show, I think, is that it is important not to confuse one or another metaphysical interpretation of the notion of objectivity (for example, the idea that we can make sense of talk of things "as they are in themselves") with the ordinary idea that our thoughts and beliefs refer to things in the world.

The diagnosis that I have suggested of Rorty's predicament is that he is so troubled by the lack of a *guarantee* that our words represent things outside themselves that, finding a guarantee of the only kind he envisages to be "impossible," he feels that he has no alternative but to reject the very idea of representation as a mistake. (Here we also see that Rorty is a disappointed metaphysical realist.) The problem, it seems to me, is that Rorty has failed to explore the sort of "impossibility" that is at issue when he concludes that such a guarantee is impossible. Rorty is right in saying that it makes no sense to think of standing outside of one's thoughts and concepts and comparing "reality as it is in itself" with those thoughts and concepts. How could *that* idea make sense? What Rorty has done is to move from the unintelligibility of this sort of guarantee to a skepticism about the possibility of representation in a perfectly everyday sense. He leaves us with the conclusion that there is no metaphysically innocent way to say that our words represent things outside themselves. By having failed to inquire into the character of the unintelligibility that vitiates the metaphysical sort of realism he attacks, Rorty remains blind to the way in which his own rejection of metaphysical realism partakes of the same unintelligibility. I say, "partakes of the *same* unintelligibility"; for if it is unintelligible to say that we *sometimes* succeed in representing things as they are in themselves, then it is equally unintelligible to say that we *never* succeed in representing things as they are in themselves. The way in which skepticism is the flip side of the craving for an unintelligible kind of certainty is illustrated by Rorty's willingness to give up the perfectly obvious fact that language can represent something that is itself outside of language. The true task of philosophy here is to illuminate the ordinary notion of representation (and of a world of things to be represented), not to rest frozen in a gesture of repudiation that is as empty as what it repudiates.

SOME REDUCTIONIST OBJECTIONS TO DEWEY'S VALUE THEORY

By "reductionist" objections to Dewey's position I mean not simply criticisms of Dewey's own views, but more generally defenses of a sharp fact/value dichotomy as something inseparable from modern scientific sophistication.[9] These defenses of the fact/value dichotomy are of two kinds: epistemological and ontological, or more simply, metaphysical. The oldest and crudest of the epistemological defenses of the fact/value dichotomy I have seen put forward like this: "How could there be 'value facts'? After all, we have no sense organ for detecting them. We can say how we detect *yellow* since we have eyes, but what sense organ do we have for detecting value?"

The weakness of this argument lies in its naiveté about perception. Perceptions of yellow may, indeed, be minimally conceptually informed, although even color perception seems to presuppose a process of acquiring the ability to discriminate the colors from one another and not just the possession of eyes. But consider the parallel question: "How could we come to tell that people are *elated*? After all, we have no sense organ for detecting elation." The fact is that we can tell that other people are elated, and sometimes we can even *see* that other people are elated. But we can only do so after we have acquired the *concept* of elation. Perception is not innocent; it is an exercise of our concepts, an exercise of what Kant called our "spontaneity."[10] Once I have acquired the concept of elation, I can see that someone is elated, and similarly, once I have acquired the concept of a friendly person, or a malicious person, or a kind person, I can sometimes see that someone is friendly, or malicious, or kind. To be sure, such judgments are fallible, but pragmatists have never believed in infallibility, either in perception or anywhere else. As Peirce once put it, in science we do not have or need a firm foundation; we are on swampy ground, but that is what keeps us moving.

Connected with the idea that to know that there are values we would need to have a special sense organ is the empiricist phenomenology according to which perceptual experience (as opposed to "emotion") is value neutral and values are added to experience by "association." (In a variant of this idea—one equally wedded to separate mental "faculties"—"perception" supplies "reason" with neutral facts, and values come from a faculty called "the will.") This phenomenology (or empiricist psychology), too, has been sharply criticized by a number of authors, not all of them pragmatists by any means.[11] But pragmatists in particular have always emphasized that experience *isn't* "neutral," that it comes to us screaming with values. In infancy we experience food and drink and cuddling and warmth as "good" and pain and deprivation and loneliness as "bad"; as our experiences multiply and become more sophisticated, the tinges and shades of value also multiply and become more sophisticated. Think, for example, of the fantastic combinations of fact and value in a wine taster's description of a wine.

However, Dewey does not make the error of supposing that merely being valued, as a matter of experiential fact, suffices to make something valu*able*. Indeed, no distinction is more insistent in Dewey's writing than the distinction between the *valued* and the valu*able*. Dewey's answer to the question, "What makes something valu*able* as opposed to merely being valued?" in a word, is *criticism*. Objective value arises, not from a special "sense organ," but from the *criticism of our valuations*. Valuations are incessant and inseparable from all of our activities, including our "scientific" ones; but it is by intelligent reflection on our valuations, intelligent reflection of the kind that Dewey calls "criticism," that we conclude that some of them are warranted while others are unwarranted. (Philosophy, by the way, is described by Dewey as *criticism of criticism!*)

This leads to the next question: "By what criteria do we decide that some valuations are warranted and some are unwarranted?" With this question, we enter more sophisticated levels of the epistemological issue. It is convenient to distinguish three parts to Dewey's answer:

(1) In judging the outcome of an inquiry, whether it be an inquiry into what are conventionally considered to be "facts" or into what are conventionally considered to be "values," we always bring to bear a large stock of both valuations and descriptions *that are not*

in question in that inquiry.[12] We are never in the position imagined by the positivists, of having a large stock of factual beliefs and no value judgments, and having to decide whether our first value judgment is "warranted," of having to infer our very first "ought" from a whole lot of "ises."

(2) We neither have nor require one single "criterion" for judging warranted assertibility in ethics (or the law) any more than we do in any other area. In particular, the authority of philosophy is not the authority of a field vested with knowledge of such a criterion or set of criteria. As Dewey himself put it, "As philosophy has no private store of knowledge or methods for attaining truth, so it has no private access to good. As it accepts knowledge and principles from those competent in science and inquiry, it accepts the goods that are diffused in human experience. It has no Mosaic or Pauline authority of revelation entrusted to it. But it has the authority of intelligence, of criticism of these common and natural goods."[13]

(3) With the appearance of the term, "intelligence," we come to the last part of Dewey's answer to the "By what criteria?" question. If Dewey does not believe that inquiry requires "criteria," in the sense of algorithms or decision procedures, either in the sciences or in daily life, he does believe that there are some things that we have *learned* about inquiry in general *from* the conduct of inquiry. Writing on Dewey, Ruth Anna Putnam and I have insisted that if one thing distinguishes Dewey as an ethicist or a meta-ethicist (the whole normative ethics/metaethics distinction tends to collapse for pragmatists), it is his emphasis on the importance of and his consistent application of the idea that *what holds good for inquiry in general holds for value inquiry in particular.*[14]

But what does hold good for inquiry in general? We have learned, Deweyans insist, that inquiry that is to make full use of human intelligence has to have certain characteristics, including the characteristics that I have referred to by the phrase "the democratization of inquiry."[15] For example, intelligent inquiry obeys the principles of what Habermasians call "discourse ethics"; it does not "block the paths of inquiry" by preventing the raising of questions and objections or by obstructing the formulation of hypotheses and criticism of the hypotheses of others. At its best, it avoids relations of hierarchy and dependence; it insists upon experimentation where possible, and observation and close analysis of observation where experiment is not possible. By appeal to these and kindred standards, we can often *tell* that views are irresponsibly defended in ethics and the law as well as in science.

Not everyone will be convinced, I know. Some of the undergraduates in a class I taught have suggested that belief in giving reasons and actually observing how various ways of life have functioned in practice, what the consequences have been, discussing objections, and so on, is just "another form of fundamentalism"! The experience of these students with *real* fundamentalism must be rather limited. Anyone who has seen real fundamentalists in action knows the difference between insisting on observation and discussion and the repressive and suppressive mode of conducting discussion that is characteristic of fundamentalism. But, in any case, I think that this objection was both anticipated and adequately responded to by the founder of pragmatism, Charles Sanders Peirce, in "The Fixation of Belief."[16] The discovery that inquiry that is to be successful in the long run requires both experimentation and public discussion of the results of that experimentation is not something a priori, but is itself something that we learned from observation and experimentation with different modes of conducting inquiry: from the failure of such methods as the method of tenacity, the method of authority, and the method of appeal to allegedly a priori reason.

In recent years, however, there has been a curious turn in the discussion. The sorts of epistemological issues that I have been dealing with were almost the only ones that figured in debates concerning the fact/value dichotomy, at least in Anglo-American philosophy, until the late 1960s. In recent decades, however, a different issue has come to the fore; more and more frequently we encounter the claim that *even if it is true that we can distinguish between an intelligent discussion in ethics and discussion that is prejudiced, closed-minded, and so on, still there cannot* really *be such a thing as warranted assertability in ethics, because there can only be warranted assertability where there is objective truth, and* (according to a number of recent thinkers) *there are good metaphysical grounds for saying that there cannot be such a thing as objective truth in ethics.*[17] The grounds in a nutshell are that the only truly objective truths there are are the truths of physics, and the alleged truths of ethics simply do not "fit" into the world picture of physics. This move fails, however, because (to use Kantian language) one thing physics cannot do is account for its own possibility. If the only facts there are are indeed the facts of physics, then there cannot be semantical facts. For example, semantical facts have proved as resistant to physicalist treatments as have ethical and legal facts. While British philosophers in particular have recently been entranced by the question of what does and what does not fit into the "absolute conception of the world" (a currently popular way of referring to future completed physics), I do not think that this particular intellectual temptation is one that this audience is likely to feel very strongly, and I shall not deal with it further here.[18]

TRUTH AND WARRANTED ASSERTIBILITY

With this last metaphysical issue, however, I come to the topic, truth and justification in the law. I have just said something about warranted assertibility in ethics and the law. I have said that we can apply standards of inquiry that we have learned from experience are necessary to the intelligent prosecution of inquiry in *any* area, and that, since we are never in the position of starting *ex nihilo* in ethics any more than anywhere else, or in the law any more than anywhere else, there is no reason that it should be impossible to discover in individual problematical situations—however fallibly—that one putative resolution is superior to another. But what is the relation of *truth* to this sort of warranted assertability?

The question is enormously difficult and delicate. At one time, I myself believed that truth could be defined as warranted assertability under "ideal" (that is to say, *good enough*) conditions, where what are good enough conditions is itself something that we are able to determine in the course of inquiry.[19] I no longer think that this works, or indeed that one need define truth at all, although I think there is a great deal philosophically to be said about the use of the word "true" and the complex relations between truth and the various semantical and epistemological notions we have. But here I want to make just one point: even if one believes that truth sometimes transcends warranted assertibility (even warranted assertibility under ideal conditions), it would be a great mistake to suppose that truth can always transcend warranted assertibility under "ideal" (or good enough) conditions.

It may be the case, for example, that some statements about the cosmological universe are such that they could be true, but there are no conditions under which we could verify that they are true; the very notion of "ideal conditions" for verifying them may not make sense. For example, it may be true that there do not happen to be any intelligent extraterrestrials anywhere, but it may be impossible to verify that this is the case. On the other hand, if the statement that there are chairs in this room is true, then of course that is something that can be verified if conditions are good enough. In fact, on the occasion of my giving the lecture from which this chapter is taken, the conditions were good enough and the statement was verified. The supposition that truth, even in such a familiar case, might in principle be impossible to verify, that we might all be "brains in a vat," or in Descartes's version, that we might all be deceived by an evil demon, has only the appearance of sense. For the supposition in question has the (usually unnoticed) feature that if we were really out of touch with the world in one of these ways, then the assumption (which is, of course, an essential part of the supposition in question) that our referential powers extend so far as to enable us to understand the conjecture that we are all brains in a vat or disembodied minds deceived by an evil demon would be false. The ability to refer to things is not something that is guaranteed by the very nature of the mind, as Descartes mistakenly supposed; reference to things requires information-carrying interaction with those things, and that is enough to rule out the possibility that truth is in all cases radically independent of what we can verify. Truth cannot be so radically non-epistemic.[20]

These are dark issues. But it is not necessary to take a position on the question as to whether truth can ever be totally recognition transcendent in order to recognize that in such familiar cases as talk about the furniture in the room truth is not recognition transcendent, that truth does entail warranted assertibility if conditions are sufficiently good. This is even more the case, I believe, when the subject matter is ethics or when the subject matter is the law. Even a hard-line metaphysical realist must agree that some subject matters are such that their very nature entails that if the statement in question is true, then the statement can, under certain conditions, be verified. This is the case, for example, with predications of intelligibility. If I say that a text is intelligible, then part of what I mean is that it can be understood, and if one understands a text then, *pace* Derrida, one can know that one understands it. (*Perfect* understanding, whatever that might be, is not, of course, at issue here.) It does not involve any version of idealism to hold that for the predicate "intelligible," truth does not transcend warranted assertibility under good enough conditions. But in the same way, I argue, there is no reason to suppose that one cannot be what is called a "moral realist" in meta-ethics, that is, hold that some "value judgments" are true as a matter of objective fact, without holding that moral facts are or can be recognition transcendent facts. If something is a good solution to a problematical human situation, then part of the very notion of its being a good solution is that human beings can recognize that it is. We need not entertain the idea that something could be a good solution although human beings are *in principle unable to recognize that it is*. That sort of rampant Platonism is incoherent.

Moral realism should not become what I just called "rampant Platonism," in addition, it need not and should not represent a commitment to the idea that there is some final set of moral truths (or, for that matter, legal truths), all of which can be expressed in some fixed moral or legal vocabulary.[21] An essential part of the "language games" that we play in science, in morals, and in the law is the invention of new concepts, and their introduction into general use; new concepts carry in their wake the possibility of formulating new truths. If the idea of a frozen "final truth" does not make sense in science, it is even more the case that it does not make sense in ethics and the law. But in contrast to most of the familiar forms of postmodernism, pragmatists do not conclude that therefore we cannot speak of truth or warranted assertability or even of objectivity.

SUMMING UP

Before I close, it may be well to sum up some of the conclusions that I have reached. I have argued that both in the case of ethics and in the law we are non-mysteriously able to observe that certain things have certain value properties: that a wine is "full bodied" and has a "rich bouquet," that a person is "refreshingly spontaneous"[22] or "compassionate," that a legal brief is "sloppily put together." This is not perception that is based simply on hardwired groups of neurons, as color perception has sometimes been supposed to be (there is still a lot of debate going on about this), but that involves the application of concepts; I have argued that all perception is of this kind. In addition, from the fact that all perception involves concepts, and concepts are always subject to criticism, it follows that perception itself is not an incorrigible "given" but subject to criticism. Inquiry does not end with perception, but the fact that perception sometimes turns out to be wrong doesn't mean that we are never justified in trusting it. Pragmatists believe that doubt requires justification just as much as belief, and there are many perceptions that we have no real reason to doubt. (This combination of fallibilism with antiskepticism is, indeed, one of the chief characteristics of American pragmatism.)[23] By Dewey's account, the judgment that something is valuable, in particular, requires not just an experience of the kind that he calls a valuing, but also requires the activity that he calls "criticism" (Dewey also uses the term "appraisal"). Furthermore, I have argued that in criticism the question "But how should we proceed?" is not the "stumper" it is sometimes supposed to be. We do know something about how inquiry should be conducted, and the principle that what is valid for inquiry in general is valid for value inquiry in particular is a powerful one. In this connection, I mentioned the principle of *fallibilism* (do not regard the product of any inquiry as immune from criticism), the principle of *experimentalism* (try out different ways of resolving problematical situations, or if that is not feasible, observe those who have tried other ways, and reflect carefully on the consequences), and the principles that together make up what I called "the democratization of inquiry." I have suggested that, in our actual lives, we are able to distinguish between warranted and unwarranted judgments (including judgments of value) at least some of the time—of course there are hard cases and controversial cases, and will continue to be—and the fact that we can distinguish between warranted and unwarranted judgments is enough. (As John Austin famously remarked, "Enough is enough; enough isn't everything.")[24] There is no recognition transcendent truth here; we need no better ground for treating "value judgments" as capable of truth and falsity than the fact that we can and do treat them as capable of warranted assertibility and warranted deniability.

7 | VALUES AND NORMS

I FIRST MET JÜRGEN HABERMAS when I lectured in Frankfurt in the summer of 1980. Since then I have followed his work with admiration and interest and to my profit. I don't have to say that that work is enormously rich and covers an immense terrain. Indeed, on the two occasions that I have given seminars on Habermas's writing, I have invited philosophically minded sociologists to co-lead the seminar with me—Dan Bell and Geoffrey Hawthorn on one occasion, and Seyla Ben-Habib on another—because Habermas's work bursts the boundaries of any one established academic discipline. I have also met Habermas in person many times, and my admiration for him as a thinker and as a human being has continued to grow. He is one of the giants of European thought in our time.

In recent years, one topic in particular has come up whenever the two of us have had the opportunity to meet. That topic is the sharp separation that Habermas posits between "values" and "norms."[1] In Habermas's writing (as in mine) there has been a number of changes of both position and emphasis through the years, but this separation is one thing that has remained constant at least since the publication of his magnificent *Theory of Communicative Action* in 1981.

By a "norm" Habermas understands a universally valid statement of obligation. Although the treatment of norms is "Kantian" in that the binding power of the norms that Habermas has spent his life defending, the norms of "discourse ethics," is identified with the binding power of rational thought and communication itself, "values," in contrast, are treated naturalistically. They are seen as contingent social products that vary as the different "life worlds" vary. Where the constraint of morality enters in connection with values is, so to speak, at the "metalevel." The Habermasian norm of "communicative action" requires us to *defend* our values by means of communicative action—fundamentally, this means in the spirit of recognizing the other as an end and not only as a means, to use the language of Kant's ethics. Only values that can survive such a defense are legitimate.[2] But among the values that are legitimate, there cannot be *better* and *worse* in any sense that transcends the "life world" of a particular group. As I have put it in our conversations (being, I admit, deliberately provocative): "Jürgen, on your account, values—as opposed to 'norms'—are as noncognitive as they are to positivists!"

An example may clarify what the disagreement was about. The last time we spent a few days together, Habermas asked me to give an example of a value (one that is not a "norm" in his sense) that I believe to represent more than my preference or the preference of some life-world or other to be right in the sense of representing how life-worlds themselves *ought* to be. I replied by saying, "I believe that, other things being equal, a world in which there are a variety of (morally permissible) conceptions of human flourishing is better than one in which everyone agrees on just one conception."

In short, although *diversity of ideals* is obviously not a "norm" in the Habermasian sense, I claim that, other things being equal, a world in which there is this kind of diversity is *better.* "Values" do not have to be global in this way; the judgment that a particular act is kind or cruel, or that a person is impertinent or refreshingly spontaneous,[3] or that a child is "having problems" or "discovering her identity"— there are endlessly many examples and endlessly many *sorts* of example—are all judgments of *value* in the sense under discussion. I maintain that such judgments are in practice regarded as true or false and *should* so be regarded.

Recently I noticed that a similar rejection of "substantive value realism" appears in the writings of another philosopher I admire, my good friend and Harvard colleague Christine Korsgaard. (Evidently there is something in Kantianism that pushes philosophers in this direction.)

In discussing the issue here, I shall proceed in the following way. First I will give a brief description of Habermas's position as I understand it. Then I will go on to question the "norm/value" dichotomy and finally to argue that skepticism about "value realism," even if restricted to values that are not "norms," is fatally self-undermining.

A BRIEF DESCRIPTION OF HABERMAS'S POSITION

I said above that for Habermas there is basically only one binding universal norm, the norm of communicative action. I assume that the notion of "communicative action" is familiar to my readers, but just to refresh memories I remind that "communicative action" is the term Habermas applies to speech and other forms of communication governed by the ideal of rational discourse. All of the specific elements that Habermas discerns in communicative action— for example, that it is governed by the norm of *sincerity,* the norm of *truth-telling,* and the norm of asserting only what is *rationally warranted*—are ways of spelling out that ideal. In addition, and again this will be familiar, communicative action is contrasted with *manipulation*. But it is not quite accurate to say that the universal norm of communicative action is the *only* valid universal ethical norm for Jürgen Habermas. At this point, I want to give a somewhat more nuanced account.

Before I do that, let me report a remark of Jürgen's. He made the remark in Frankfurt a few years ago, in the discussion that followed a lecture I gave. What he said was that, "We need some categorical imperatives, *but not too many.*" What he meant, I am sure, is that, on the one hand, the condemnation of unspeakable acts (think of all the torture and genocide that have gone on and are still going on in our world) requires a strong distinction between conduct that is merely "not nice" and conduct that is unconditionally *wrong*—and that is what any "norm," any universal deontological statement, aims to give us. It is, on the other hand, necessary to restrict such imperatives to what I call the "meta-level," restrict them to a plane in which what they prescribe—permit me to use somewhat vague terms—is something like a *democratic constitution* for ethical discussion, because once we start writing a large number of specific commandments that are supposed to be universally binding to all human beings, we run the danger of authoritarianism. It is because of this fear of "too many" (and too specific) universal ethical norms, I think, that Jürgen Habermas often writes *as if* the only universal norm were communicative action. But of course it cannot be.

It cannot be the case that the *only* universally valid norm refers solely to *discourse*. It is, after all, possible for someone to recognize *truth-telling* as a binding norm while otherwise being guided solely by "enlightened egotism." (This is, indeed, the way of life that was recommended by the influential if amateurish philosophizer—I cannot call her a philosopher—Ayn Rand.) But such a person can violate the spirit if not the letter of the principle of communicative action at every turn. After all, communicative action is contrasted with *manipulation,* and as such a person can manipulate people without violating the maxims of "sincerity, truth-telling, and saying only what one believes to be rationally warranted." Ayn Rand's capitalist heroes manipulated people all the time (even if she didn't consider it manipulation) via their control of capital, for example. Indeed, the person who says, "do what I want or I'll shoot you," need not be violating any maxim concerned solely with *discourse*. But it would be a mistake to use such examples as objections to Habermasian "discourse ethics."

It would be a mistake because without question the maxim of engaging in communicative action itself operates within the framework of Kant's categorical imperative. Habermas certainly believes that one must act so as to treat the other always as an end, and not as a mere means. This is what the rational egotist violates (Ayn Rand's rejection of altruism is precisely a rejection of this formulation of the categorical imperative). But the objection to Kant's categorical imperative has always been that it is difficult to derive specific rules of conduct from it. The charge, repeated endlessly since Hegel, that Kantian ethics is empty formalism, is an extreme version of this objection.

While other contemporary philosophers of a Kantian bent— John Rawls and, more recently, Christine Korsgaard and Barbara Herman, among others—have tried to rebut this charge by deriving contentful ethical rules within a broadly Kantian framework, Habermas has adopted a different tack. Assuming that we have the minimum prerequisite for an ethical life at all—that is, assuming we have a community of human beings who *do* regard the ends of others as important, and who do not simply assume that their own ends should override—Habermas's approach is to assume that disagreement about what the ethical life *concretely* requires of us is a fact of life, something that will not go away.

Habermas is certainly right that disagreements about values (as well as disagreement about norms of conduct) will always be with us (barring a totalitarian suppression of all thought worthy of the name). The idea that it should be the task of philosophy to deliver an *ex cathedra* resolution of all our moral disagreements is absurd. As Michele Moody-Adams has recently put it:

> "An effective challenge to . . . skepticism about the relevance of moral theory to moral life must begin by relinquishing the vain insistence upon the authoritative status of philosophical moral inquiry . . . There is a middle way between the skeptical anti-theorist view on which moral philosophy should be *replaced* by some other discipline—such as cultural anthropology, or experimental psychology, or literature, or some combination thereof—and the unsupportable view that moral philosophy is the final court of appeal on questions of moral justification. That middle way involves thinking of moral philosophy as a valuable and distinctive participant in the ongoing process of moral inquiry."[4]

One way of understanding Habermasian "discourse ethics" is to think of it as precisely such a "middle way," a way in which philosophy can be a "valuable and distinctive participant" in our ethical discussions without pretending to the authority of a "final court of appeal." (Many, perhaps most, of the silly criticisms of discourse ethics that I have run across depend on the double mistake of supposing that Habermas believes that an "ideal speech situation" will actually be *reached* at some particular time in the future and supposing that such a situation is precisely the "final court of appeal" that Moody-Adams rightly rejects.) Rather than undertake the task of producing a "final" ethical system, a final set of rules of conduct, what Habermas offers us instead is a rule for how to conduct our inevitable disagreements over the first-order rules that should govern our conduct. In this respect, we might describe Jürgen Habermas as a "minimalist Kantian moral philosopher."

I have expressed my belief in the *value* of discourse ethics in a number of places.[5] It is not my purpose to enter here into the controversy as to whether a discourse ethics is really *all* that one can get from a broadly Kantian approach. My question is rather whether Kantian universal norms, be they many or few, can really exhaust what is "objective" in ethics, or whether, on the other hand, there is sometimes something more to "values" than the contingencies of the histories of various local "life worlds."

THE "NORMS/VALUES" DICHOTOMY IS PROBLEMATIC

In this section I shall (temporarily) put Habermas to one side, and consider a different sort of "Kantian" view. But I have not forgotten that this is a chapter dealing with Habermas, and I shall return to his thought in later sections.

The sharpest statements of a stark reductive naturalism with respect to what I am calling values that I know of are found in Christine Korsgaard's chapters in *The Sources of Normativity*[6] and her replies to critics explaining and defending the views set forth in the chapters she subsequently published under the title "Motivation, Metaphysics, and the Value of the Self" in the journal *Ethics*.[7] In those replies she writes (p. 52): "As I read him [Kant] he does not accept any sort of substantive value realism. He does not think that the objects of our inclinations are good in themselves. We do not want things because we perceive that they are good: rather our initial attractions to them are natural psychological impulses."

What Korsgaard calls "the objects of our inclinations" are not yet "values" according to her account, nor are these "initial psychological impulses" yet valuations. We *make* them into values and valuations by adopting a maxim that directs us to value them or not to value them, to act on them or not to act on them. She writes, "The larger point here is that in Kant's theory *our values* are created from psychological materials, from the natural bases of interest and enjoyment, rather than from nothing. Here as elsewhere in Kant's theory reason works by imposing form on matter that it finds" (p. 57).

But in "imposing form on matter that it finds," reason is guided by no substantive ends. Thus Korsgaard writes (p. 60), "There is really only one principle of practical reason—the principle that we should choose our maxims as universal laws." And making it plain that she is speaking for herself, and not just as a Kant-interpreter,

Korsgaard writes (pp. 60–61), "I argue for the conclusion that human beings must see ourselves as value-conferring and must therefore value humanity as an end in itself."

The problem that I find with such formulations arises from the following simple reflection: Our "maxims," and the "laws" that we impose upon ourselves by universalizing them, themselves *contain value terms,* in particular the so called "thick ethical words" that I discussed in Chapter 2—words such as "kind," "cruel," "impertinent," "sensitive," "insensitive," and so on. For instance, it is a rule of conduct (implicitly if not explicitly) for every decent human being (one that none of us succeeds in always obeying, perhaps, but nonetheless a rule of conduct that we aspire to living up to) that one should treat those one deals with, and especially those in distress or trouble, with *kindness* unless there is an overriding moral reason that one should not. Similar rules of conduct direct one to avoid *cruelty,* to avoid *impertinence,* to avoid *humiliating* others, to be *sensitive* to the thoughts and feelings of others, and so on.

In an early book criticizing both Sartrean existentialism *and* logical positivism,[8] Iris Murdoch suggested that philosophers of both kinds share a picture of the mind as divided into discrete "faculties,"[9] a picture in which perception supplies "neutral" facts and values comes from the will. This is, of course, not (or anyway not *exactly*) the Kantian picture, but in Korsgaard's version—perhaps in all versions?—that picture *also* assumes a faculty psychology, one in which "our initial attractions" to "the objects of our inclinations" are "natural psychological impulses," while our values (*all* our values, even those that we would normally ascribe to self-love) come from autonomous reason.[10] (This is, of course, just Kant's famous dichotomy between inclination and reason.) But, contrary to this picture, terms like "kind," "sensitive," "cruel," "humiliated," "impertinent"—terms that, as I argued in Part I, cannot be "factored" into a "valuative component" and a "descriptive component" describable in "value neutral" terms—do not stand for neutral descriptive properties, properties that our "natural psychological impulses" encounter without the benefit of what McDowell, reviving Aristotle's notion, calls an acquired "second nature."[11] The fact that an act is cruel or kind, sensitive or insensitive, pert or refreshingly spontaneous, is available only through the lenses of *value concepts*. Contrary to the Kantian picture, in our moral lives we cannot and do not get by with a vocabulary obtained by supplementing a starkly naturalistic vocabulary with a single moral notion (the notion needed to indicate that one is "imposing the form of law on psychologically generated incentives," say *ought*).[12] Without our human manifold of *values*, there is no vocabulary for *norms* (Korsgaard's "laws") to be stated *in*.

BERNARD WILLIAMS'S WAY OUT

Ever since writing *Reason, Truth, and History*, I have argued along the lines that value terms are both conceptually indispensable and irreducible to merely descriptive terms.[13] In *Ethics and the Limits of Philosophy*, Bernard Williams simultaneously *conceded* this and attempted to *neutralize* its philosophical significance.[14] Instead of concluding as I did in *Reason, Truth, and History* (p. 145) that "Ethics does not *conflict* with physics, as the term 'unscientific' suggests; it is simply that 'just' and 'good' and 'sense of justice' are concepts in a discourse which is not *reducible* to physical discourse ... *other* kinds of essential discourse are not reducible to physical discourse and are not for that reason illegitimate. Talk of 'justice' like talk of 'reference' can be *non*-scientific without being *unscientific*," Williams defended the views that (1) only the concepts of science describe the Furniture of the World, and that (2) the only truly "scientific" concepts are those of *physics*.[15]

Williams's strategy was to say that while the "thick" ethical concepts are indeed not factorizable into separate descriptive and evaluative components, the statements we make using them have no "absolute" validity ("absoluteness" is a central notion in Williams's metaphysics). However, ethical statements *can* properly be called "true," according to Williams, because "true" is an adjective we are able to use when we are speaking "within some social world or other," as well as when we are speaking "absolutely."[16]

It isn't, Williams is careful to make clear, that one and the same ethical statement can be "true in culture A" and "false in culture B." It is rather that the "truth" of the ethical statement can only be talked about *within* the "social world" in which the statement was made. Other cultures are "disbarred" from so much as considering the statement (unless there is a "real option" of going over from one culture to the other—but my purpose here is not to go into the intricacies of Williams's scheme).[17]

For our purposes, the following observation will suffice: even if Williams's view were coherent, it could hardly help a Kantian like Korsgaard. For if our ethical maxims contain thick ethical concepts—as they obviously do—then making them into "universal laws" will be problematic in any view according to which *what the extensions of those ethical concepts are* is a question that has no universally intelligible answer. Any view according to which *just which acts, persons, things, fall under those concepts* is a question that only makes sense "within some social world or other." The "laws" that my reason "legislates" could still possess *formal* universality, perhaps, but their *content* would be anything but "universal." Relativism of any kind with respect to values cannot leave "norms" (maxims upon which reason has imposed "the form of law," in Korsgaard's terminology) unaffected.

DOES "DISCOURSE ETHICS" AVOID THIS PROBLEM?

In the years that I have known Habermas, his position has changed in certain respects, so I am not quite certain how he would respond today to the points I just made.[18] But there are two possible responses that I should like to discuss (very likely Habermas's actual response will turn out to be different from both).

Consider a case in which a thick ethical concept is used in my "social world" but not in yours. For example, there are today social worlds in which the concept "chastity" is never used (except, perhaps, with "shudder quotes"). If one of my norms is, "Avoid unchaste behavior," and this norm makes no sense to you because the concept "unchaste" is simply an anachronism from your point of view, what are we to do if Williams is right and we cannot suppose that there is a social-world-independent extension of the concept?

Well, one thing we could do is discuss the question: "Ought you to acquire this concept?" If the answer to that question is "yes," we could discuss the question: "Ought you to accept the norm I just framed using that concept?" as well, of course, as the question: "Should I abandon the concept altogether?"[19]

The problem this poses for discourse ethics is that *discussion* (as opposed to *negotiation*) presupposes that the question at issue is cognitively meaningful. If we suppose it is not, then as Ramsey remarked, such a "discussion" "consists in A saying he would feel guilty if he weren't constant, B saying *he* wouldn't feel guilty in the least."[20] It is precisely by appreciating the necessity of discourse ethics that we can appreciate how fatal it is to Habermas's own philosophical-political project to make any concessions to what we might call "sociologism about values"—to treat value disputes as, in effect, mere social conflicts to be resolved (although they are frequently that too) and not as *rational disagreements calling for a decision as to where the better reasons lie.*[21] Even if our maxims employ vocabularies as different as can be, we can engage in discussion (in the normative sense of "communicative action") with the aim of coming to a common vocabulary and a common understanding of how that vocabulary should be applied. However unless there is such a thing as a correct answer to those questions, that discussion cannot really be an effort to find the answer for which there are *better reasons*. At best the discussion can be an exercise in what Richard Rorty, a philosopher I am sure Habermas does not agree with, calls "continuing the conversation." Can it be the case that the only universally valid ethical rule is "Keep talking"? Answer "yes" (this is the first response that I mentioned) and you have "minimalist ethics" with a vengeance.

The second response is suggested by the way in which Habermas defended discourse ethics *before* he published his *Theory of Communicative Action*—defended it with the aid of Karl Otto Apel's "transcendental pragmatics."[22] (The *Theory of Communicative Action* itself seems to "wobble" from the Apel position to a more "minimalist" position, on my reading.) The heart of Apel's position is that, following Peirce,[23] it identifies truth with *what would be agreed upon in the limit of indefinitely continued discussion* (in the normative sense of "discussion"—communicative action—of course). Apel's important move is to apply this identification also to *ethical claims*, indeed to *all* discourse.[24]

If we accept this idea, then we can assert that if, on the one hand, continued discussion in the widest possible community (sometimes identified by both Habermas and Apel with the community of "all those affected") leads to the conclusion that no resolution of the disagreement is possible, then the contested concept (in our case, "chastity") should be dropped. For in that case, *there is no truth at all on either side,* since if there *were* truths (or valid statements) about either (a) which actions are chaste and which unchaste, or (b) whether one should universalize the maxim "Avoid unchaste behavior," then those truths would eventually be agreed on by all participants to the (ideal) discussion we envisaged *because that is the very meaning of "true."*[25] If, on the other hand, there *are* truths about (a) and (b), then again by the very definition of "true," sufficiently continued discussion *must* (under ideal conditions) converge on them.

Let us note the very substantial difference between the Apelian response to my question and the first, minimalist, response. The minimalist response, as I described it, simply accepts the view of Bernard Williams that I discussed in Chapter 2, to the effect that value claims stated in thick ethical language possess only a relative sort of validity—validity in "some social world" or other (Williams himself would also say that statements of *norms* also possess only relative validity, but this, of course, Habermas could not accept). The minimalist response simply tells us how to behave in the absence of such a thing as a universally valid claim about value. In the Apelian view, in contrast, such claims *can* have universal validity, and discourse ethics provides the procedure by which we can find out (in the long run) which ones do have it.

In order to see whether this view is adequate, let us consider two questions:

(1) Is Apel right in endorsing Peirce's definition of truth?

(2) If, as I shall argue, the answer to the first question is that Peirce's definition of truth is not correct for descriptive statements, including statements of physical science, could it nevertheless be correct for *ethical* statements?

APEL AND PEIRCE HAVE A WRONG THEORY OF TRUTH

However one might try to make the Peirce-Apel account more acceptable by contemporary standards of clarity (and counterfactuals about what would happen if discussion went on forever or were indefinitely prolonged, hardly count as clear), one feature is essential to it: on such an account, *it is metaphysically impossible for there to be any truths that are not verifiable by human beings.* The account is thus a species of what is today called "antirealism" because it makes the limits of what can be true of the world dependent on the limits of human verification-capacities.

To discuss realism and antirealism here would require a lengthy digression. I will only state my view, which I have defended elsewhere at length, summarily.[26]

The argument for antirealism always takes the form of an accusation, the accusation that the idea that *truths may sometimes not be verifiable, even ideally,* is unbearably "metaphysical." (Antirealism never admits that *it* is a form of metaphysics.) Yet if I say that "it may be impossible to ever know the facts of Moses' life," it is hard to see that this is a *metaphysical* utterance. It would rather seem to be the claim that there are no truths about Moses' life except what we and other people *in the future* could verify is the "metaphysical" claim, in the sense in which metaphysics is almost by definition contrary to common sense. It is, on the contrary, part of both science and common sense, and deeply imbedded in the world views of both science and common sense, that it is a wholly contingent question whether every truth could, even "in principle," be learned by beings such as ourselves, and it is deeply imbedded in the theories of present-day science that for a number of reasons the answer to that question is that, as a matter of contingent empirical fact, there are *many* truths that are beyond the power of our species to ascertain.[27] Although I myself tried for a number of years to defend the idea that truth can be identified with "idealized rational acceptability," I am today convinced that this was an error.[28] If "transcendental pragmatics" is the working out of the consequences (or alleged consequences) of an antirealist theory of truth, then it is a working out of the consequences of a *mistake,* and should be abandoned.

AN APELIAN ACCOUNT OF ETHICAL TRUTH, AND ITS DIFFICULTIES

Earlier I raised the question, "If Peirce's definition of truth is not correct for descriptive statements, including statements of physical science, could it nevertheless be correct for *ethical* statements?" The question is serious because while it is, as I just pointed out, deeply built into both our best commonsensical and scientific pictures of the world that some empirical statements are impossible to verify and also built into both the commonsense realism and the scientific realism that goes with those pictures that this unverifiability is no reason at all to say that they are neither true nor false, the opposite is the case with ethical statements. Ethicists have long insisted that our duties are *knowable* by us, and that, indeed, if they were not they could not be our duties. But this by itself does not mean that Apel's theory of truth can be saved (for my purposes here) by simply restricting it to ethical claims.

As I see it, the critical issue is the justification of the step from saying that any true claim about our duties is "knowable by us" to "would be the outcome of an ideal discussion, if that discussion were sufficiently prolonged." Explaining why that step is problematic will bring me back to my original topic, the way in which "values" and "norms" are intertwined. I shall break the critical issue up into three problems.

(1) An ideal discussion is one in which all the participants accept the norm of engaging in communicative action with all that that entails: speaking honestly, trying one's best to say what is true, trying one's best to say what is justified, trying to win one another over by the force of argument and not by manipulation of any kind, and so on. Since all of the norms and maxims of discourse ethics are built into the description of the ideal discussion situation, they will, by the very definition of the situation, be accepted by all the participants. But then *their* justification—and they constitute essentially the whole of Habermasian ethics—*isn't* that they are the *outcome* of an indefinitely prolonged Peircean inquiry at all!

Apel's response to this in various books and papers was to say that they are justified by a "transcendental justification," namely that they are *presupposed* by rationality, presupposed by the procedures which define what it is to pursue truth.[29] If we restrict the definition of truth as the product of an ideal consensus to ethical statements, then the transcendental argument will have to be similarly restricted. The claim will then be that the norms and maxims of discourse ethics are presuppositions of *ethical* rationality. I am inclined to agree with this but for Deweyan rather than Peircean reasons.[30] In any case, I wish to set aside possible objections at this stage. I will only note that even if following the norms of discourse ethics is (were) a *necessary condition* for arriving at justified ethical beliefs, what Apel needs to show is something much stronger; he needs to show that conformity to those norms is also a *sufficient condition* for arriving at justified (and ultimately at *true*) ethical beliefs. This leads to the other problems I said I would raise.

(2) Even if we prescind from problems about the unclarity of counterfactuals of the form "if discussion were indefinitely prolonged." Do we have any clear conception of a world in which people are able to discuss an issue *forever?* I shall now argue that *there is no reason to believe that the outcome of an ideal and sufficiently prolonged discussion of an ethical question would inevitably be correct.*

My skepticism about this claim of Apel's (and, I am afraid, of Habermas's as well) can be explained with the aid of an analogy. To describe the analogy I have in mind, let me first describe a brief discussion in Wittgenstein's *Philosophical Investigations* (II, 207ff.).

Wittgenstein considers disputes about whether someone is "feigning" an emotion. (One example he uses is a dispute about whether someone is really smitten by love.) I may be sure that my judgment on such a question is right, but I may not be able to convince other people. What he says, quite reasonably, is that such judgments, judgments on which the community does not come to agreement, may nevertheless be right. Some people have more *Menschenkenntnis* (understanding of people) than others, and *Menschenkenntnis* cannot be reduced to a system of rules.

Wittgenstein does say that people who have more *Menschenkenntnis* are, in general, better at making prognoses; but he does not say, nor does he imply, that *every individual correct judgment* of the genuineness of an emotion will eventually be confirmed behaviorally in a way that would command the assent of the whole community. Instead he says that such judgments are typically made on the basis of "imponderable evidence."

Consider now (this is my analogous ethical dispute) a dispute as to whether an act is cruel. A father engages in psychological cruelty by teasing his child, while denying (either because he is obtuse or because of a streak of sadism) that the child's tears are really "serious." "He has to learn to take it," the father says.

Will the whole community come to agreement that this constitutes cruelty? *Must* they come to agreement, even if the speech situation is "ideal"? (The analogous questions in the case of Wittgenstein's example would be: will the whole community come into agreement that the person's signs of attraction constitute being really smitten with love? *Must* they come into agreement, even if the speech situation is "ideal"? Indeed, isn't the distinction between being *really* in love and not really being in love itself an *ethical* distinction?)

Here we have to proceed very delicately. Suppose most of the members of the community, or even a significant minority, share the father's obtuseness in the case described. They are not, we suppose, bad people in most other respects. They genuinely want to do what is right, and they love rational argument. Indeed, they regard the question as to whether the case is a case of "cruelty" as a fascinating one, and they discuss it endlessly, No one tries to manipulate anyone else, and everyone listens patiently to everyone else's arguments. But we can perfectly well imagine that the father and others like him never "get it." There is no consensus, although on a straightforward construal of the requirements of an ideal speech situation (speaking honestly, trying one's best to say what is true, trying one's best to say what is justified, trying to win one another over by the force of argument and not by manipulation of any kind, and so on) the speech situation may well be "ideal."

Obviously, Apel and Habermas are going to cry "foul." But before I consider their response, or the response(s) I anticipate from Habermas at least, let me state the point I want to make with such examples.

What is wrong with the discussants in the above situation *isn't* that they aren't obeying the norms of discourse ethics. What is wrong is stateable *using the thick ethical vocabulary appropriate to the particular ethical problem.* They are "obtuse" (the opposite of having *Menschenkenntnis*), they have a "trace of sadism," and so on. To describe what an "ideal discussion situation" would be in this case, one would have to use (and presuppose one's audience had mastered) *thick ethical concepts.*

In *The Theory of Communicative Action*, it seems at times as if Habermas, at least, wants to build in the additional requirement that, in effect, the participants in an ideal discussion have achieved the equivalent of an ideal psychoanalysis (whether through actual psychoanalysis or otherwise).[31] But even if one believes, as I do, in the reality of psychoanalytic insight, psychoanalysis never claimed to make the subject into a perfect *Menschenkenner* (nor would psychoanalysts claim that they themselves are ideal *Menschenkenner*).[32]

That something like psychoanalysis might be the solution may be suggested, in the case of my example, by my use of the scientific-sounding expression "a trace of sadism." But it is not the case that all failures in moral perception can be described or explained using such scientific-sounding expressions. By "moral perception," let me make clear, I do not mean the sort of thing that ethical intuitionists such as G. E. Moore talked about, a mysterious faculty for perceiving a "non-natural property" of goodness. I mean the ability to see that someone is, for example, "suffering unnecessarily" as opposed to "learning to take it," that someone is "being refreshingly spontaneous" as opposed to "being impertinent," that someone is "compassionate" as opposed to being "a weepy liberal," and so on and on. There is no *science* that can teach one to make these distinctions. They require a skill that, in Iris Murdoch's words, is "endlessly perfectible," and that as she also says, is interwoven with our (also endlessly perfectible) mastery of moral vocabulary itself.[33]

At this point, I think, I arrive at *a fundamental ambiguity in Habermas's position.* If Habermas will, as I am trying to persuade him to do, *restrict the claims of discourse ethics;* if, specifically, he will say that discourse ethics is a *part* of ethics, a valuable and important part to be sure, but not one that can stand on its own, not *the* foundation (or the foundation in "modernity") of *all* the "validity" that ethics can possess, then, I believe, he will be on very much the right track. But if one attempts to defend the more ambitious claims that he and Apel have made on behalf of discourse ethics, then either *there will be no reason to believe the claims* (this will be the case if "discourse ethics" is restricted to some definite set of norms that are supposed to characterize reason) or the claims will be *empty*. For if the claim that the correct verdict in an ethical dispute will be arrived at in an ideal speech situation just means that it will be arrived at *if the disputants are ideally morally sensitive, imaginative, impartial, and so on,* then the claim is a purely "grammatical" one; it provides no content to the notion of a "correct verdict in an ethical dispute" that that notion did not independently possess. Indeed, not only are "ideally morally sensitive" and other such concepts, themselves *ethical* concepts, but giving them content in any actual dispute will require "thickening" them, replacing them with terms that are still *value* terms but that have more descriptive content.

The problem, I suggest, is built into the Kantian approach. Kantiantism, as we saw in Christine Korsgaard's work, looks for principles characteristic of practical reason itself, while treating values as either mere psychological facts ("natural psychological impulses") or as the product of the action of practical reason on those mere psychological facts. Korsgaard's difficulty in accounting for the "automatic standing" of self-love illustrates how this survival of Kant's notorious inclination/reason dichotomy absolutely blocks one from seeing the way in which thick ethical concepts defy all the traditional fact/value dichotomies.[34]

(3) There is an objection I recall having once seen Lyotard make against Habermasian discourse ethics, to the effect that discourse ethics marginalizes or excludes the "inarticulate." In one sense, this objection is unfair, but I believe that thick ethical concepts have to

be used to explain *why* it is unfair. If what Lyotard meant was that a community of articulate and intelligent language users might consciously agree in an ideal discourse situation that it was right for them to *exploit* and manipulate less articulate members of the community, then the charge is unfair because the action of such a group with respect to the "inarticulate" members of the community would be manipulative. For a discussion to be ideal in the Habermasian sense it is not enough that those who do the arguing obey the principles of discourse ethics in their arguments *with one another;* even those who do not speak up must be regarded as members of the group (otherwise it does not include all affected persons), and every member of the group must have a non-manipulative attitude towards every other. With respect to those who are unable to argue well, there is always William James's beautiful demand that we "listen to the cries of the wounded." One does not have to be articulate to cry out! If the cries of the wounded are ignored, then the speech situation is certainly not "ideal" in a Habermasian or Apelian sense.

It is possible, however, that Lyotard had something different in mind. It is very likely that what he envisaged was the possibility of a discussion in which those who are articulate do have good will towards the inarticulate, at least subjectively, and do hear at least the most obvious "cries of the wounded." But one can have good will, at least subjectively, and systematically misinterpret those cries, and do so in one's own interest. If this is indeed what Lyotard was thinking of, then this is just another special case of the previous problem.

WHY DO PEOPLE WANT TO RELATIVIZE OR "NATURALIZE" VALUES ANYWAY?

Although the desire to "naturalize" ethics is extremely widespread, the "price" of naturalization is extremely high. (Contrary to Dewey's usage, I am using "naturalism" and its derivatives as synonymous with materialism, because regrettably, that is how the word has come to be used.) All naturalist accounts have in common that they either deny that ethical sentences are expressions of *judgments*, of thoughts that can be described as true and false, warranted and unwarranted, without some such "rider" as "in the relevant social world," or "relative to the individual's desires and attitudes," or (if they do agree that there are such things as fully rational and objective ethical judgments) they give an account of the *purpose* (and sometimes of the *content*) of such judgments in *nonethical* terms. In the latter case, whether the account be evolutionary (so that ethical judgments are ultimately in the service of "altruism," which is itself conceived of merely as a mechanism to insure group survival), or utilitarian (so that ethical judgments are calculations of utility from the point of view of a group or species or even—for example, in the case of Peter Singer—many species), or contractarian (so that ethical judgments serve an interest to "give reasons" that are themselves appraisable, at least behind a "veil of ignorance," without presupposing a specifically *ethical* point of view, or appraisable presupposing only impartiality), ethics is, in effect, treated as something that is to be justified from *outside*.

I think that in our time this may reflect the seductive but ultimately disastrous attractiveness of a strategy that also led to logical positivism. That strategy might be described thus: "Give the skeptic almost everything he claims, as long as you can keep a certain bare minimum." In the philosophy of science, what this strategy led to was the idea that we can concede to the skeptic that we have no knowledge of unobservables as such, no knowledge even of the existence of tables and chairs and objects independent of our sensations, no knowledge even of the existence of other people, certainly no ethical or metaphysical or aesthetic knowledge, as long as we can hold on to the claim that we have knowledge of our own sensations (sometimes this was restricted to our own sensations at the present moment).[35] The thought was that this bare minimum would allow us to retain the idea of predictive knowledge and hence of science. Today the attraction of this point of view seems to have declined as mysteriously as it rose (but one can never be sure it will not assert itself again in the future).

In the case of ethics, the corresponding thought is that we can concede to the skeptic that we have no *irreducibly* ethical knowledge. But what is, what could be, *more* irreducible than my knowledge, face to face with a needy human being, that I am *obliged* to help that human being? (Even if, on reflection, I decide that other *ethical* obligations override that first obligation, this does not change my awareness of something absolutely fundamental and irreducible. As long as one treats that obligation as a mere "feeling," one will wander in a place (whether it looks like a desert landscape or like a tropical jungle) far outside the ethical world.[36]

The two cases, the case of ethics and the case of philosophy of science, are moreover, not unrelated for as I remarked earlier hypothesis selection in science presupposes epistemic values, and the terms for these values—"coherent," "simple," "beautiful" (applied to a theory), and the like behave just like the "thick ethical terms."[37]

Indeed, as I will argue in the next and last chapter, each and every one of the familiar arguments for relativism (or contextualism) with respect to ethical values could be repeated in connection with these epistemic values. Rather than accept those arguments in *either* case, what we need to do is to recognize that both ethical values and epistemic values are indispensable in our lives. Indeed, the arguments that are supposed to show the impossibility of "unnaturalizable" values *prove too much*—indeed, the demand that we accept only what we can give a reductive account of would, I have claimed in many of my books, lectures, and papers, eliminate not only value-talk, but talk of reference[38] as well as talk of causality,[39] talk of counterfactuals,[40] and much besides. Something is indeed wrong here, but it is reductionism (*alias* "naturalism") that is wrong and not value-talk.

I know that I will be reminded that Habermas is not a logical positivist, nor a reductionist, nor even a "naturalist." But it seems to me that at bottom his desire to treat all value discourse *outside* the narrow limits of discourse ethics as mere negotiation of differences between "life words," and also the reason that he fears conceding any objectivity that goes beyond this to such value discourse— namely that such a concession would not be compatible with "modernity" (meaning here the modern suspicion of everything that is supposed to be "metaphysical")—are, at bottom, *positivistic* desires and reasons. The idea that one can concede so much to the positivists and still retain a tiny bit that, it is thought, will be suffi- cient to rebuild all the ethical objectivity that one wants or needs is an error in exactly the way that the positivist idea that one can con- cede so much to the skeptics and still retain a tiny bit that, it was thought, would be sufficient to rebuild all the scientific objectivity that one wants or needs was an error.

CONCLUSION

Of course, there are reasons other than fear of being thought too "metaphysical" for worrying about recognizing so many irreducible values. I've already quoted Habermas as saying, "We need some categorical imperatives, but not too many." But accepting that ethi- cal values can be rationally discussed and need not be "naturalized" is not the same thing as accepting apriorism or authoritarianism with respect to values. Ever since liberal societies rejected the ap- peal to revelation as a foundation for our ethical and political life, we have been ethical fallibilists, and indeed, the principle Ruth Anna Putnam and I have attributed to John Dewey, the principle that "what applies to inquiry in general applies to ethical inquiry in particular," requires us to be fallibilists, given that fallibilism has be- come an inseparable part of the methodology of rational inquiry in general.[41] But fallibilism is not all that rational inquiry in general re- quires, and discourse ethics, *Habermasian* discourse ethics, can and should be seen (or so I have long urged) as spelling out in more detail what rational inquiry worthy of the name requires. Recognizing that there must be *more* to ethics than discourse ethics in no way diminishes the importance of discourse ethics.

I have often remarked to friends that in ethics we need both Aristotelian and Kantian insights, and I never cease to be astonished at the resistance I meet when I say this. Again and again I am told that it is "very hard" (in a tone of voice that implies: "impossible") to reconcile a concern with human flourishing with Kantian ethics. But if what I have argued in this chapter is right, our imperfect but indefinitely perfectible ability to recognize the demands made upon us by various values is precisely what provides Kantian (or "discourse") ethics with *content*.

8 | THE PHILOSOPHERS OF SCIENCE'S EVASION OF VALUES

I REMEMBER SEEING A LETTER somewhere in which Dewey wrote that far from being just one special corner of experience, value is something that has to do with all of experience.[1] In the philosophy of science, what this point of view implies is that value judgments are essential to the practice of science itself. Here I do not refer only to the kind of value judgments that we call "moral" or "ethical": judgments of "coherence," "plausibility," "reasonableness," "simplicity," of what Dirac famously called the "beauty" of a hypothesis, are all value judgments in Charles Peirce's sense, judgments of what he called the "admirable" in the way of (scientific) conduct. (For Peirce, aesthetics—which he conceived of in a way heavily influenced by Kant's critique of judgment—is the abstract theory of the admirable; ethics, as the abstract theory of the admirable in the way of conduct, presupposes aesthetics, and logic, or the theory of inquiry, or the theory of the admirable in the way of scientific conduct, presupposes ethics.)[2]

In thinking about what I might discuss in this chapter, it occurred to me that, first of all, this issue—the way in which value judgments are presupposed by scientific inquiry—has been a preoccupation of mine for many years, and second, that it would be of interest to survey the ways in which so many leading philosophers of science have tried to avoid admitting that this is the case. Indeed, the issue, although raised emphatically by every one of the pragmatists, has been dealt with so cursorily by the mainstream philosophers of science, that (mimicking my friend and colleague Cornel West's title *The American Evasion of Philosophy*), I decided to title this "The Philosophers of Science's Evasion of Values."[3] I shall discuss a number of philosophers in the order in which they figured in my own life and thought.

First, however, I have to point out that my very first introduction to philosophy of science was in my undergraduate years when I studied with C. West Churchman at the University of Pennsylvania. Churchman was a pragmatist himself and certainly did not evade the fact that science presupposes value judgments. Indeed, I remember him writing on the blackboard the following four propositions, which he attributed to his teacher A. E. Singer Jr. who was a former student of William James:

(1) *Knowledge of (particular) facts presupposes knowledge of theories* (under which term Singer included all generalizations). For example, to know that something is an oak tree is to know that it belongs to a kind of tree (a notion which is itself connected with many generalizations) that generally has leaves with a certain shape, that usually produces acorns, and so on. Here Singer was attacking the idea that science can "start" with bare particular data and build up to generalizations by induction and abduction. There is no such thing as a "start" in this sense, Singer was saying; we always already presuppose a stock of generalizations when we do science.

(2) *Knowledge of theories* (in the wide sense described) *presupposes knowledge of (particular) facts.* This would be denied by Kantians who would argue that certain generalizations are a priori.

(3) *Knowledge of facts presupposes knowledge of values.* This is the position I defend. It might be broken into two separate claims: (i) that the activity of justifying factual claims presupposes value judgments, and (ii) that we must regard those value judgments as capable of being *right* (as "objective" in philosophical jargon), if we are not to fall into subjectivism with respect to the factual claims themselves.[4]

(4) *Knowledge of values presupposes knowledge of facts.* (Against all philosophers who believe that [some part of] ethics is a priori.)

After I graduated from the University of Pennsylvania in 1948, I did graduate work at Harvard for one year and then transferred to UCLA, where I received my Ph.D. in 1951. Although the view that fact and value interpenetrate was defended at Harvard by Morton White, who had also taught me at the University of Pennsylvania and who was responsible for encouraging me to go to graduate school—he moved to Harvard in 1948—I quickly came under the influence of Quine, and subsequently at UCLA, under that of Hans Reichenbach, both of whom regarded value judgments as completely noncognitive. How did these two mighty thinkers evade the whole issue of the role of values in science?

In Quine's case, when I was a graduate student at Harvard in 1948–1949 and in the years immediately afterward ("On What There Is" had been published; "Two Dogmas of Empiricism" was not to be published until 1951, but the doctrines in that article were already the subject of conversation in Emerson Hall), Quine's statements on epistemology were ones of which William James might well have approved. For example, Quine wrote: "our statements about the physical world face the tribunal of sense experience not individually but only as a corporate body."[5]

And again, in the concluding section of that famous paper: "Each man is given a scientific heritage plus a continuing barrage of sensory stimulation; and the considerations which guide him in warping his scientific heritage to fit his continuing sensory promptings are, where rational, pragmatic."[6]

Perhaps the best statement of Quine's overall picture, however, is in another famous paper, "Carnap and Logical Truth."[7] The last paragraph of that paper, which presents Quine's famous doctrine that fact and convention interpenetrate without there ever being any sentences that are true by virtue of fact alone or true by virtue of convention alone, reads in full: "The lore of our fathers is a fabric of sentences. In our hands it develops and changes, through more or less arbitrary and deliberate revisions and additions of our own, more or less directly occasioned by the continuing stimulation of our sense organs. It is a pale grey lore, black with fact and white with convention. But I have found no substantial reasons for concluding that there are any quite black threads in it, or any white ones."

These pragmatist-sounding utterances might well lead one to think that Quine ought to be friendly to a similar doctrine that fact and value interpenetrate in science. In Chapter 2 of this book I quoted Vivian Walsh to roughly this effect.[8] Indeed, Quine's close friend Morton White tried to convince Quine of this in the 1950s but in vain.[9] For, although it continued to be true of Quine that, as an empiricist he continued to think of the conceptual scheme of science, ultimately, as a tool for predicting future experience in the light of past experience,[10] Quine's discussions of the problem of theory selection came more and more to be couched in utterly unrealistic terms. He came to write[11] as if the problem were that assuming we are given the totality of true sentences of the form, "If $P_1(x,y,z,t)$, then $P_2(x',y',z',t')$," where P_1 and P_2 are observation predicates and where the quadruples of coordinates name space-time points (call such sentences "observational conditionals"), how can we select among theories that predict all (or as large a subset as possible) of these? More precisely, Quine worried about the questions: (1) Could there be two bodies of total science (two alternative "conceptual schemes of science") that imply the same set of true observation-conditionals (and no false ones)—part of the unreality of Quine's discussion is that probabilistic prediction never enters into the picture—and that cannot be shown to be one and the same theory in different disguises?[12] And (2): If there could be, how could one choose between them? This is, needless to say, not the problem of theory selection that faces any actual scientist! (Note that Quine never tells us how we are supposed to know that all the observation-conditionals implied by these alternative theories are true.) In fact, this is epistemology from the point of view of Logically Omniscient Jones, and then only if Logically Omniscient Jones has an "oracle" that informs her of the truth-value of observation-conditionals.

I don't want to suggest that Quine has no response to this sort of criticism. His answer to those who want a more realistic epistemology, an epistemology that concerns how real scientists manage to select real theories on real data, is the famous, "Why not settle for psychology?"[13] What many of his readers have missed is that when Quine said this he *meant* it. "Naturalized epistemology" in Quine's sense means the *abandonment* of epistemology. "Psychology" (which for Quine, always means Skinnerian psychology) is all the epistemology we want or need. This is evasion of the epistemological question with a vengeance!

My next teacher after I left Harvard in 1949, Hans Reichenbach, was a very different sort of philosopher. What Reichenbach tried to show was that all epistemology could be reduced to iterated and concatenated applications of one simple rule (often called the "straight rule" of induction). The rule can be stated thus: Calculate the relative frequency r of Bs among the so far observed As, and posit that the relative frequency of Bs (or the limit of the relative frequency of Bs, if there are infinitely many As) among *all* the As, including the future ones, is r ± ε where "ε" is an arbitrarily selected margin of acceptable error.

There are four problems with this, however, each of them important, interesting, and worthy of very extended discussion. The first, which I have discussed at length elsewhere,[14] is simply that the straight rule is inconsistent. The second is that even if Reichenbach had succeeded in reducing induction to such a rule (to some consistent version of such a rule), all that he would be able to claim for it is that it would converge to the right hypothesis (about the frequency of various Bs in various populations A) *in the long run*. The problem of a rule for selecting hypotheses in "real time" remains completely open in Reichenbach's work (as he was well aware, by the way). The third problem, which will come up again below, is that his denial of the need for what Peirce called "abduction" (and other philosophers of science call "the hypothetico-deductive method") depended upon the idea of putting theories into reference classes and running simple straight-rule inductions on those classes, and this, as Ernest Nagel showed in an important monograph, is utterly unrealistic.[15] The fourth, and by no means the least interesting or important, problem has to do with Reichenbach's incredible (though, in my view, praiseworthy) metaphysical ambition.[16] Reichenbach wanted not only to reduce all induction to one rule, but he claimed to have *a deductive "vindication" of that rule;* that is, a deductive proof that the straight rule must succeed if any method at all is able to succeed. In short, Reichenbach wanted to "solve Hume's Problem," as he understood that problem. (I have shown, by the way, that the very feature of Reichenbach's straight rule that makes it inconsistent is essential to the "vindication" argument; one cannot have a consistent rule that admits a Reichenbachian "vindication.")[17] In the process of "vindicating" induction (as he believed he had done), Reichenbach needed, however, to assume that he had available observation statements that themselves had no predictive import (otherwise "induction" would have had to be already used to verify the observation statements, leading to an infinite regress). But Reichenbach himself, in a beautiful debate with C. I. Lewis, argued (correctly in my view) that there are no such observation statements.[18] In sum, Reichenbach agreed with A. E. Singer Jr.'s claim that "Knowledge of (particular) facts presupposes knowledge of theories (that is, of generalizations)," but his "vindication argument" tacitly presupposed the falsity of this claim.

In 1953, after a year on a Rockefeller Fellowship and a one-year teaching post at Northwestern University, I joined the Princeton faculty as an assistant professor, and I immediately met Rudolf Carnap, who was visiting at the Institute for Advanced Study. Carnap was as warm and welcoming as he was brilliant, and in spite of the difference in our ages and ranks (which meant nothing whatsoever to Carnap), we became warm friends. Carnap's way of avoiding (or evading) the idea for which I have been contending, the idea that values—epistemic values, such as "coherence," "plausibility," "reasonableness," "simplicity," "elegance" and the like—are presupposed in the activity of selecting scientific theories, was to try to show that science proceeds by a formal syntactic method. To put it very briefly, Carnap wanted to reduce theory choice to an algorithm. But the only algorithms he was able to devise were limited to very simple sampling problems (such as estimating the relative frequency of red balls in an urn given a sample of balls selected from the urn). Today no one holds out any hope for Carnap's project.[19]

Karl Popper (who I met much later, and only once or twice) rejected the very idea of inductive logic (in fact, he thought empirical science needs only deductive logic and observation), but he, too, hoped to reduce the scientific method to a simple rule: test all strongly falsifiable theories and retain the ones that survive. But that doesn't work either. When a theory conflicts with what has previously been supposed to be fact, we sometimes give up the theory and we sometimes give up the supposed fact, and as Quine famously put it in a passage I quoted earlier, the decision is a matter of trade-offs that are "where rational, pragmatic"—and that means (although Quine, of course, doesn't say so) a matter of informal judgments of coherence, plausibility, simplicity, and the like.[20] Nor is it the case that when two theories conflict, scientists wait until the observational data decide between them, as Popperian philosophy of science demands they should.

An example I have often used in this connection is the following: both Einstein's theory of gravitation and Alfred North Whitehead's 1922 theory (of which very few people have ever heard) agreed with special relativity, and both predicted the familiar phenomena of the deflection of light by gravitation, the non-Newtonian character of the orbit of Mercury, the exact orbit of the Moon, among other things.[21] Yet Einstein's theory was accepted and Whitehead's theory was rejected fifty years before anyone thought of an observation that would decide between the two. Indeed, a great number of theories *must* be rejected on non-observational grounds, for the rule "Test every theory that occurs to anyone" is impossible to follow. As Bronowski once wrote to his friend Popper, "You would not claim that scientists test every falsifiable theory if as many crazy theories crossed your desk as cross mine!"[22]

In short, judgments of coherence, simplicity, and so on are presupposed by physical science. Yet coherence, simplicity, and the like are values. Indeed, each and every one of the familiar arguments for relativism in ethics could be repeated in connection with these epistemic values. The argument that ethical values are metaphysically "queer" because (among other things) we do not have a sense organ for detecting "goodness" could be modified to read "epistemic values are ontologically queer because we do not have a sense organ for detecting simplicity and coherence." The familiar arguments for relativism or noncognitivism from the disagreements between cultures concerning values (arguments that are often driven by the fashionable, but I believe wholly untenable, pictures of different cultures as "incommensurable") could be modified to read that there are disagreements between cultures concerning what beliefs are more "coherent," "plausible," "simpler as accounts of the facts," and so on; and in both the case of ethics and the case of science, there are those who would say that when cultures disagree, saying that one side is objectively right is mere rhetoric.[23]

I have just emphasized the fact that familiar arguments for relativism with respect to values would, if they were correct, apply to our epistemic values as well because it is only by appreciating this that one can see just how self-refuting relativism actually is. Consider, for example, the well-known views of Richard Rorty, who holds that we should scrap the whole notion of an objective world and speak of views that "our culture" would accept (sometimes he adds "at its best") instead. This view that all there is to values—including the epistemic values—is the consensus of "our" culture presupposes that at least some of our commonsense claims can be accepted without philosophical reinterpretation of the kind proposed. For instance, talk of "cultures" only makes sense when talk of other people, talk of beliefs, in short, the idea of a common world, is already in place. If Rorty were to say that talk of other people is just "marks and noises" that help *him* "cope," it would become obvious that his talk of "the standards of our culture" is empty by his own lights. Commonsense realism about the views of my cultural peers coupled with anti-realism about everything else makes no sense. If, as Rorty likes to claim, the notion of an objective world makes no sense, then the notion of "our culture" cannot be more than Rorty's private fantasy, and if there is no such thing as objective justification—not even of claims about what other people believe—then Rorty's talk of "solidarity" with the views of "our culture" is mere rhetoric.

Rorty, of course, would agree with my claim that scientific inquiry presupposes that we take seriously claims that are not themselves scientific, including value claims of all kinds; he would simply say that we should give up the notion that there is such a thing as objectivity either in scientific or nonscientific inquiry. But at least some philosophers who wish to hold on to the idea of scientific objectivity without admitting that science presupposes judgments that are not themselves scientific would take a different tack.

The most commonly advocated alternative, in fact, to admitting that the existence of warrantedly assertible claims as to matters that are non-scientific, warrantedly assertible claims as to what is *more plausible* than what, warrantedly assertible claims as to what is *more coherent* than what, warrantedly assertible claims as to what is *simpler* than what—are presupposed by the activity of gathering knowledge even in the paradigm science of physics is the "reliabilist" epistemology proposed by Alvin Goldman.[24] According to that epistemology, what makes a belief in science justified is that its acceptance was arrived at by a method which is "reliable" in the sense of having a high probability of resulting in the acceptance of true hypotheses. Effective objections have been made to this idea, and Goldman has made sophisticated alterations in his original formulations in order to meet them, but these are not the grounds on which I would argue that this approach does not succeed. To see why, let us simply consider the question: "On what 'method' was Einstein relying when he accepted the special and general theories of relativity?"

Einstein's own views are well known. He tells us that he arrived at the special theory of relativity by *applying an empiricist critique to the notion of "simultaneity"* and that he arrived at general relativity by *seeking the "simplest" theory of gravity compatible with special relativity in the infinitesimal domain.* We know that the physicists who accepted these two theories also regarded these as compelling considerations in their favor. Both of these methods are *completely topic specific* (so much so, that the reference class of theories involved is much too small for it to make sense to speak of "probabilities" here at all), and both of these methods presuppose judgments of reasonableness.[25] And judgments of reasonableness simply do not fall into classes to which we are able to assign probabilities.[26] In sum, not only is there no reason to think that the sorts of judgments I have been talking about—judgments of reasonableness—can be reduced to non-normative judgments; there is not even a serious sketch of such a reduction.

CONCLUSION

I have argued that even when the judgments of reasonableness are left tacit, such judgments are presupposed by scientific inquiry. (Indeed, judgments of coherence are essential even at the observational level: we have to decide which observations to trust, which scientists to trust—sometimes even which of our memories to trust.) I have argued that judgments of reasonableness can be objective, and I have argued that they have all of the typical properties of value judgments. In short, I have argued that my pragmatist teachers were right: "knowledge of facts presupposes knowledge of values." But the history of the philosophy of science in the last half century has largely been a history of attempts—some of which would be amusing, if the suspicion of the very idea of justifying a value judgment that underlies them were not so serious in its implications—to evade this issue. Apparently any fantasy—the fantasy of doing science using only deductive logic (Popper), the fantasy of vindicating induction deductively (Reichenbach), the fantasy of reducing science to a simple sampling algorithm (Carnap), the fantasy of selecting theories given a mysteriously available set of "true observation conditionals," or, alternatively, "settling for psychology" (both Quine)—is regarded as preferable to rethinking the whole dogma (the last dogma of empiricism?) that facts are objective and values are subjective and "never the twain shall meet." That rethinking is what pragmatists have been calling for for over a century. When will we stop evading the issue and give the pragmatist challenge the serious attention it deserves?

NOTES

PREFACE

1. One should not be put off by the forbiddingly technical-sounding title of Walsh's *Rationality, Allocation and Reproduction* (Oxford: Clarendon Press, 1996). Imagine the title to be simply "Rationality and Economics"! In my opinion, this is a must-read for anyone interested in the question. Also, I cannot resist recommending Walsh's delightful early book, *Scarcity and Evil* (Englewood Cliffs, N.J.: Prentice-Hall, 1961).

INTRODUCTION

1. The reader will find references in the notes to the individual chapters of this volume.
2. See the quotations in Chapter 3.

THE EMPIRICIST BACKGROUND

1. The three touchstones of an analytic judgment for Kant were (1) that its negation yielded a contradiction (and thus ran into conflict with *the* basic law of logic: the principle of non-contradiction), (2) that its

subject contained its predicate, and (3) that is was explicative rather than ampliative (in other words, that it did not extend our knowledge but only made implicit knowledge explicit). Kant took it for granted that any judgment that possessed one of these three features would also possess the other two. But once Frege recasts the distinction between analytic and synthetic judgments in the light of his own contributions to logic, these three features can no longer be taken to coincide. In particular, (2) falls away as a hopeless criterion for assessing the status of all judgments (since Frege shows that not all judgments have a subject/predicate structure); and (3) will no longer do, since Frege is precisely concerned to mark his difference from Kant by claiming that, although the truths of arithmetic are, by his lights, analytic, nonetheless, they do extend our knowledge. What makes a truth analytic for Frege is his successor version of (1): namely, that it can be logically derived from (what he calls) "the basic laws of logic." (For the difference between Frege and Kant here, see endnote 61, in James Conant, "The Search for Logically Alien Thought," in *The Philosophy of Hilary Putnam, Philosophical Topics*, 20, no. 1 [Spring 1992], p. 172.) The logical positivists, following Wittgenstein in the *Tractatus,* tried to combine Frege's claim (as against Kant) that mathematical truths are analytic, while agreeing with Kant (against Frege) that all analytic judgments are merely explicative and not ampliative.

2. See "Objectivity and the Science/Ethics Distinction," collected in my *Realism with a Human Face* (Cambridge, Mass.: Harvard University Press, 1990), pp. 163–178.

3. I first argued this in "The Refutation of Conventionalism," collected in my *Philosophical Papers,* vol. 2: *Mind, Language and Reality* (Cambridge: Cambridge University Press, 1975), pp. 153–191. See also my "Convention: A Theme in Philosophy," collected in *Philosophical Papers,* vol. 3: *Realism and Reason* (Cambridge: Cambridge University Press, 1983), pp. 170–183.

4. "True on the basis of the L-rules alone" is Carnap's characterization of the analytic sentences on p. 432 of "Testability and Meaning," *Philosophy of Science,* 3, no. 4 (1936), pp. 419–471; and 4, no. 1 (1937), pp. 1–40.

5. I am omitting the role of Frege in this story, on whose work the positivists sought to build, while shifting his original conception of what it is for a proposition to be analytic.

6. W. V. Quine, "Carnap and Logical Truth," in P. A. Schilpp, ed., *The Philosophy of Rudolf Carnap* (LaSalle, Ill.: Open Court, 1963), p. 405.
7. Ibid., p. 406.
8. "Two Dogmas of Empiricism," in W. V. Quine, *From a Logical Point of View* (Cambridge, Mass.: Harvard University Press, 1953), pp. 20–46. An earlier version appeared in *Philosophical Review* (January 1951).
9. "The Analytic and the Synthetic," collected in Hilary Putnam, *Philosophical Papers*, vol. 2: *Mind, Language and Reality*, pp. 33–69.
10. Quine does this with the aid of what he calls "a socialized concept of stimulus synonymy." See W. V. Quine, *Word and Object* (Cambridge, Mass.: MIT Press, 1960), pp. 55–57.
11. This is precisely the function that Rudolf Carnap called on the notion of the analytic to perform: "Mathematics, as a branch of logic, is . . . tautological. In the Kantian terminology the sentences of mathematics are analytic. They are not synthetic a priori. Apriorism is thereby deprived of its strongest argument. Empiricism, the view that there is no synthetic a priori knowledge, has always found the greatest difficulty in interpreting mathematics, a difficulty which Mill did not succeed in overcoming. This difficulty is removed by the fact that mathematical sentences are neither empirical nor synthetic a priori but analytic." See Carnap, "The Old and the New Logic," originally published in German, in volume 1 of *Erkenntnis* (1930–1931), reprinted in translation in A. J. Ayer, ed., *Logical Positivism* (New York: Free Press, 1959), pp. 60–81.
12. I speak of the analytic (as conceived by Carnap and his successors) as "inflated" because it was stretched to include all of mathematics together with (by various authors) principles about the topology of time and so on.
13. Although Hume nowhere says exactly this, the principle "no *ought* from an *is*" has almost universally been taken to be the upshot of the "observation" with which Hume concludes the *Treatise*, Book III, Part 1, section I (and which he says he "could not forbear adding . . . which may be found of some importance"). Hume says that in all the "systems of morality" he had met, the author would start in "the ordinary way of reasoning," proving, say, the existence of God or describing human society, and suddenly switch from "is" and "is not" to "ought" and "ought not," for example from "God *is* our creator" to "we *ought* to obey him." No explanation was ever given of this "new relation,"

and Hume makes it clear that he does not think this step can be justified. See David Hume, *A Treatise of Human Nature*, ed. L. A. Selby-Biggs and P. H. Nidditch (Oxford: Oxford University Press, 1978), pp. 469–470.

14. This was pointed out by Elijah Milgram in "Hume on Practical Reasoning" (*Treatise* 463–469), *Iyyun: The Jerusalem Philosophical Quarterly,* 46 (July 1997), pp. 235–265; and in "Was Hume a Humean?" *Hume Studies,* 21, no. 1 (April 1995), pp. 75–93.

15. Here I follow Milgram's analysis, referred to in the previous note.

16. Although Charles L. Stevenson, among others, interprets Hume as holding that value judgments are factual judgments, I believe that this is a mistake. According to Stevenson in *Facts and Values* (New Haven: Yale University Press, 1963), p. 11, Hume "in effect" defines good as "approved by most people"; in his earlier *Ethics and Language* (New Haven: Yale University Press, 1944), p. 276, Stevenson's formulation is that "Hume's manner of defining [*sic*] the moral terms makes such a statement as 'Anything is good if and only if the vast majority of people, on being fully and clearly informed about it, would have approbation for it' an analytic one." However, Hume sharply distinguishes between "a mistake of *fact* and one of *right*" in Appendix I to his *Enquiry Concerning the Principles of Morals* (numbered section 241, in Selby-Bigge's edition). See L. A. Selby-Bigge, ed., *Enquiries Concerning the Human Understanding and the Principles of Morals, by David Hume* (Oxford: Clarendon Press, 1975), p. 290. This follows the section (numbered 237 by Selby-Bigge) in which Hume asks "where is that matter of fact that we call *crime;* point it out; determine the time of its existence; describe its essence or nature; explain the sense or faculty to which it discovers itself. It resides in the mind of the person who is ungrateful. He must, therefore, feel it and be conscious of it. But nothing is there except the passion of ill will or of absolute indifference. You cannot say that these, of themselves, always, and in all circumstances, are crimes. No, they are only crimes when directed towards persons who have before expressed and displayed good-will towards us. Consequently, we may infer, that the crime of ingratitude is not any particular *fact;* but arises from a complication of circumstances which being presented to the spectator excites the *sentiment* of blame, by the particular structure and fabric of his mind" (ibid., pp. 287–288; emphasis in the original). Here, as the context merely makes clear,

what holds of "crime" is supposed to hold of "virtue" and "vice" in general: there is no matter of fact that is the virtuous or vicious character of an action. What misleads Stevenson is that Hume *also* holds that in fact the great majority of persons, if fully knowledgeable about the circumstances (and if they make a sufficient effort to view those circumstances impartially) will approve and disapprove of the same actions under the influence of "the sentiment of humanity." But this is not to say that the *idea* of a good action is the idea of an action that most people will approve of; if it were, then Hume could not say that there is no "matter of fact" here.

17. As already pointed out, this reading of Hume is one I owe to Elijah Milgram.

18. See the quotations in note 16.

19. John Rawls, "Kantian Constructivism in Moral Theory," collected in John Rawls, *Collected Papers,* ed. Samuel Freeman (Cambridge, Mass.: Harvard University Press, 1999), pp. 303–358. See also Rawls' *Lectures on the History of Moral Philosophy,* ed. Barbara Herman (Cambridge, Mass.: Harvard University Press, 2000).

20. The *locus classicus* for this version of the logical positivist account of ethics is chapter 17, "The Nature of Ethics," in Hans Reichenbach, *The Rise of Scientific Philosophy* (Berkeley: University of California Press, 1951).

21. Rudolf Carnap, *The Unity of Science* (London: Kegan Paul, Trench, Hubner, 1934), pp. 26–27.

22. Here Carnap was referring to the so-called "early" Wittgenstein of the *Tractatus.*

23. Ibid., p. 22.

24. Just what "logical consequence" should mean if we are interpreting Kant's distinction is somewhat unclear, however. For a proposal in this connection, see Chapter 5 of Hilary Putnam, *Realism and Reason,* pp. 94–95.

25. This is the title of a chapter of *The Rise of Scientific Philosophy,* mentioned in an earlier note.

26. This is not to deny that there were important differences between the logical positivists on the topic of just how "empty" statements of value are. Reichenbach differed from Carnap in insisting that ethical "judgments" are imperatives and that imperatives can "entail" other imperatives and thus (unlike arbitrary sequences of words) can stand

in logical relations to one another. Stevenson, though he insisted that emotive statements were lacking in "cognitive content," was concerned to offer what he called a "logic" of emotive discourse.

27. *Enquiry Concerning the Principles of Morals,* p. 290.

28. Cavell's pages on Stevenson in Part III of *The Claim of Reason* (Oxford: Clarendon Press, 1979), pp. 259–273, are devastating in the way they reveal that Stevenson has no ear at all for what actual ethical argument sounds like.

29. Strictly speaking, this is only true if we ignore astronomical bodies (for example, the moons of Jupiter), which are only visible with the aid of the telescope. As far as I know, Hume never discusses the status of such objects.

30. One might, of course, think that the Newtonian notion of a *gravitational force* referred to something unobservable, but Newton himself had discouraged this, writing, for example: "How these Attractions may be performed, I do not here consider. That I call attraction may be performed by impulse, or by some other means unknown to me." And Newton's follower Clarke (some would say his "spokesman") put this anti-metaphysical point of view even more strongly in his controversy with Leibniz: "It is very unreasonable to call *Attraction a Miracle* and an unphilosophical Term; after it has been so often distinctly declared, that by that Term we do not mean to express the Cause of Bodies tending *towards each other,* but barely the *Effect,* or the *Phenomenon itself,* and the *Laws* or Proportions of the *Tendency,* discovered by *Experience.* . . ." Quoted by Alexandre Koyre in *From the Closed World to the Infinite Universe* (Baltimore: Johns Hopkins Press, 1957), p. 271.

31. Reichenbach is an exception here; see "Reichenbach's Metaphysical Picture" in Hilary Putnam, *Words and Life* (Cambridge, Mass.: Harvard University Press, 1994), pp. 99–114; and Hilary Putnam, "Hans Reichenbach: Realist *and* Verificationist," in Juliet Floyd and Sanford Shieh, eds., *Future Pasts* (Oxford: Oxford University Press, 2001), pp. 277–287.

32. Cf. Carnap's account of the development of the logical positivists' views in "Testability and Meaning."

33. In Part II of "Testability and Meaning," Carnap introduced a notion of "reduction" (by extremely restricted means) and replaced the logical positivist requirement that all factual predicates be *definable* by means of observations terms with the more liberal requirement that they be

reducible to such terms. The main, indeed the only significant, effect of this liberalization was that such dispositional predicates as *soluble* could then be accepted as cognitively meaningful. The dispositional predicates in question correspond to ordinary language predicates of the form "If x were subject to test condition C (e.g., being put in water), it would have property P (e.g., dissolving)," where C, and P are themselves observation terms. ["Testability and Meaning," pp. 431–453.]

34. "The Foundations of Logic and Mathematics," in *International Encyclopedia of Unified Science*, vol. 1, part 1 (Chicago: Chicago University Press, 1938), pp. 139–214. See especially §24, "Elementary and Abstract Terms," pp. 203–209.

35. *Physics, the Elements* (Cambridge: Cambridge University Press, 1920), p. 122. For a full (and highly sympathetic) discussion of the "Campbellian" conception, see R. B. Braithwaite, *Scientific Explanation* (Cambridge: Cambridge University Press, 1946).

36. Carnap, "The Foundations of Logic and Mathematics," §24, p. 207.

37. A classic account of the problems recognized by the positivists themselves is C. G. Hempel's "Implications of Carnap's Work for the Philosophy of Science," in P. A. Schilpp, ed., *The Philosophy of Rudolf Carnap* (LaSalle, Ill.: Open Court, 1963), pp. 685–710. For a criticism of Carnap's post-1939 position, see my "What Theories Are Not" in E. Nagel, P. Suppes, and A. Tarski, eds., *Logic, Methodology and Philosophy of Science* (Stanford, Calif.: Stanford University Press, 1962), pp. 240–252. Collected in Hilary Putnam, *Philosophical Papers*, vol. 2: *Mathematics, Matter and Method* (Cambridge: Cambridge University Press, 1975), pp. 215–227.

38. Here I strongly disagree with Thomas Ricketts, who thinks that Carnap's own doctrines are free of metaphysical commitments. See Ricketts, "Carnap's Principle of Tolerance, Empiricism, and Conventionalism," in Peter Clark and Bob Hale, eds., *Reading Putnam* (Oxford: Blackwell, 1994), pp. 176–200, and my reply, ibid., pp. 280–281.

39. In his reply to Hempel's paper (cited above) in *The Philosophy of Rudolf Carnap*, pp. 958–966, Carnap speaks of "the completely interpreted terms of V_O [the 'observation vocabulary']" (p. 960), and says that "a partial interpretation" of the theoretical terms is provided by the theoretical postulates and the correspondence postulates [postulates containing both theoretical and observational terms] (p. 959).

40. Vivian Walsh tells me that this was suggested to him by William Demopolis in a personal communication.

41. Early attacks included Thomas Kuhn, *The Structure of Scientific Revolutions*, originally included in *The Encyclopedia of Unified Science*, combined edition, vol. 2 (Chicago: University of Chicago Press, 1955), and subsequently published separately (Chicago: University of Chicago Press, 1977); Norwood Russell Hanson, *Patterns of Discovery* (Cambridge: Cambridge University Press, 1958); and Hilary Putnam, "What Theories Are Not," collected in *Mathematics, Matter, and Method* (Cambridge: Cambridge University Press, 1975).

42. "The terms of V_O [the "observation vocabulary] are observable properties of events or things (e.g., 'blue,' 'hot,' 'large,' etc.) or observable relations between them (e.g., 'x is warmer than y,' 'x is contiguous to y,' etc.)." Rudolf Carnap, "The Methodological Character of Theoretical Concepts," in *Minnesota Studies in the Philosophy of Science*, vol. 1, *The Foundations of Science and the Concepts of Psychology and Psychoanalysis*, ed. Herbert Feigl and Michael Scriven (Minneapolis: University of Minnesota Press, 1956, 1976), p. 41. "An observable property may be regarded as a simple special case of a testable disposition; for example, the operation for finding out whether a thing is blue or hissing or cold, consists simply in looking or listening or touching the thing respectively. Nevertheless, in the reconstruction of the language it seems convenient to take some properties for which the test procedure is extremely simple (as in the three examples just mentioned), as directly observable and use them as primitives in L_o." Ibid., p. 65.

43. "Cruel" is not an observation disposition in Carnap's sense, because we cannot say in precisely what observable circumstances cruelty will manifest itself in precisely what observable behavior, in other words, we cannot capture the notion by a finite set of "reduction sentences."

44. Donald Davidson, *Essays on Actions and Events* (Oxford: Clarendon Press, 1960); see also Part II of Hilary Putnam, *The Threefold Cord: Mind, Body and World* (New York: Columbia University Press, 1999).

45. For example, Paul Churchland has written, "The real motive behind eliminative materialism [Churchland's program] is the worry that the 'propositional' kinematics and 'logical' dynamics of folk psychology constitute a radically *false* account of the cognitive activities of humans and of the higher animals generally. . . . The worry about propositional attitudes, in short, is that . . . they are too much like (the

avowedly nonexistent) phlogiston, caloric, and the four principles of medieval alchemy." "Activation Vectors versus Propositional Attitudes: How the Brain Represents Reality," *Philosophy and Phenomenological Research*, 52, no. 2 (1992), p. 420.

46. Today these neurological states are usually supposed to be characterized indirectly, as the "realizers" of appropriate "functional states." This is the view of David Lewis, "An Argument for the Identity Theory," in his *Philosophical Papers*, vol. 1 (Oxford: Oxford University Press, 1983), pp. 99–107.

47. This is the view that I proposed in a series of papers published between 1960 and 1975 under the name "Functionalism." (For an account of these papers and my reasons for giving up the view, see the article "Putnam, Hilary," in Samuel Guttenplan, ed., *A Companion to the Philosophy of Mind* [Oxford: Blackwell, 1994], pp. 507–513; the papers themselves are collected in Hilary Putnam, *Philosophical Papers*, vol. 2: *Mind, Language and Reality* [Cambridge: Cambridge University Press, 1975].) A similar view is defended by Jaegwon Kim in "Psychophysical Supervenience," collected in his *Supervenience and Mind* (Cambridge: Cambridge University Press, 1993). I criticize Kim's arguments (from my present point of view) in *The Threefold Cord: Mind, Body and World*, pp. 93–134.

48. This is my recollection from conversations in his house at the Institute for Advanced Studies in Princeton, where he was a Fellow in 1953–1954. He thought that for the present, at least, these states could only be characterized by their *effects*, e.g., as "the neurological state which is responsible for such-and-such behavior," where "responsible for" means "is normally the cause of," not "is invariably the cause of." This is an interesting anticipation of David Lewis's position, described in note 46.

49. Cf. Hilary Putnam, "Functionalism: Cognitive Science or Science Fiction?" in *The Future of the Cognitive Revolution*, ed. David Martel Johnson and Christina E. Erneling (New York: Oxford University Press, 1987), pp. 32–44.

THE ENTANGLEMENT OF FACT AND VALUE

1. By Hare for example, in *Moral Thinking* (Oxford: Clarendon Press, 1981), p. 16.

2. Here I neglect the small class of "observable disposition terms" mentioned in the preceding chapter as irrelevant to my topic.

3. "Two Dogmas, of Empiricism" was read to the Meeting of the Eastern Division of the American Philosophical Association in Toronto in December 1950. It is collected in Quine's *From a Logical Point of View* (Cambridge, Mass.: Harvard University Press, 1961), pp. 20–46.

4. I criticize Quine's tendency to treat mathematics as synthetic in spite of himself in two essays: "Rethinking Mathematical Necessity," and "Philosophy of Mathematics: Why Nothing Works," collected in *Words and Life* (Cambridge, Mass.: Harvard University Press, 1994).

5. Vivian Walsh, "Philosophy and Economics," in *The New Palgrave: A Dictionary of Economics*, vol. 3, ed. J. Eatwell, M. Milgate, and P. Newman (London: Macmillan, 1987), pp. 861–869.

6. Morton White, *Toward Reunion in Philosophy* (Cambridge, Mass.: Harvard University Press, 1956).

7. See *The Collected Papers of Charles Sanders Peirce*, vol. 1: *Principles of Philosophy*, ed. Charles Hartshorne and Paul Weiss (Cambridge, Mass.: Harvard University Press, 1931), §176–283, and vol. 5, *Pragmatism and Pragmaticism*, (1934), §120–150; for an extended discussion see Christopher Hookeway, *Peirce* (London: Routledge, 1992). An excellent selection of Peirce's remarks on this topic are brought together as "Philosophy and the Sciences: A Classification" in Justus Buchler, ed., *The Philosophical Writings of Peirce* (New York: Dover, 1955), pp. 60–73.

8. Roderick Firth, "Epistemic Merit, Intrinsic and Instrumental," in *Proceedings and Addresses of the American Philosophical Association*, 55, no. 1 (September 1981), pp. 5–23.

9. "Was Wittgenstein *Really* an Antirealist about Mathematics?" in Timothy G. McCarthy and Sean C. Stidd, eds., *Wittgenstein in America* (Oxford: Clarendon Press, 2001), pp. 140–194; see also "Objectivity without Objects," in Hilary Putnam, *Ethics without Ontology* (forthcoming).

10. A good account of the difficulties is John Etchemendy, *The Concept of Logical Consequence* (Cambridge, Mass.: Harvard University Press, 1990).

11. For a fuller discussion of the self-refuting character of logical positivism, see "Philosophers and Human Understanding," collected in my *Philosophical Papers*, vol. 3: *Realism and Reason* (Cambridge: Cambridge University Press, 1983), pp. 184–204.

12. Some of these—by Iris Murdoch, John McDowell, R. M. Hare, and

John Mackie—are cited in subsequent notes. In addition, I am thinking of David Wiggins's "Truth, Invention, and the Meaning of Life,"
collected in his *Needs, Values, Truth* (Oxford: Clarendon Press, 1998),
pp. 87–138, and Philippa Foot's *Virtues and Vices* (Berkeley and Los An-
geles: University of California Press, 1978), particularly, "Morality as a
System of Hypothetical Imperatives," pp. 157–173.

13. The paradigmatic "error theorist" was J. L. Mackie, *Ethics; inventing
right and wrong* (Harmondsworth: Penguin, 1978). His "error theory"
will be explained shortly.

14. The words quoted in this sentence were listed as examples by José Or-
tega y Gassett, who noticed the phenomenon of entanglement very
early. See his *Obras Completas,* vol. 6 (Madrid: Revista de Occidente,
1923), pp. 317, 320–321.

15. Hare, *Moral Thinking,* p. 74.

16. Ibid., pp. 21–22, 72–75.

17. Elizabeth Anderson, *Value in Ethics and Economics* (Cambridge, Mass.:
Harvard University Press, 1993), p. 102.

18. R. M. Hare, *Moral Thinking,* p. 72.

19. Such proponents have been around for a long time. Bernard Williams
reports that "the idea that it might be impossible to pick up an evaluative concept unless one shared its evaluative interest is basically a
Wittgensteinian idea. I first heard it expressed by Philippa Foot and
Iris Murdoch in a seminar in the 1950s." Bernard Williams, *Ethics and
the Limits of Philosophy* (Cambridge, Mass.: Harvard University Press,
1985).

20. Cf. Chapter 9 of *Reason, Truth and History* (Cambridge: Cambridge
University Press, 1981).

21. See the papers collected in Part II, "Reason, Value and Reality" of
John McDowell, *Mind, Value, and Reality* (Cambridge, Mass.: Harvard
University Press, 1998).

22. Iris Murdoch, *The Sovereignty of Good* (London: Routledge and Kegan
Paul, 1970).

23. "Non-Cognitivism and Rule-Following," chapter 10 in John McDowell, *Mind, Value, and Reality,* p. 201.

24. I consider Mackie's "queerness" argument in detail in "Pragmatism
and Moral Objectivity," in *Words and Life,* pp. 151–181.

25. J. L. Mackie, *Ethics: Inventing Right and Wrong* (Harmondsworth: Penguin, 1978), p. 41.

26. Here I repeat a point I made in "Objectivity and the Science-Ethics Distinction," in M. Nussbaum and A. K. Sen, eds., *The Quality of Life* (Oxford: Clarendon Press, 1993), pp. 143–157. Collected in Putnam, *Realism with a Human Face* (Cambridge, Mass.: Harvard University Press, 1990), pp. 163–178.

27. Bernard Williams, *Ethics and the Limits of Philosophy* (Cambridge, Mass.: Harvard University Press, 1985).

28. Bernard Williams, *Descartes: The Project of Pure Enquiry* (Harmondsworth: Penguin, 1978), p. 237. That Williams agrees with Descartes on this point is made clear on p. 241: "There is every reason to think that [the absolute conception] should leave out secondary qualities."

29. Ibid., p. 247.

30. Williams, *Ethics and the Limits of Philosophy*, p. 150.

31. Here I briefly summarize criticisms I have made of Williams "absolute-perspectival" distinction in "Objectivity and the Science-Ethics Distinction" as well as in Chapter 5 of *Renewing Philosophy* (Cambridge, Mass.: Harvard University Press, 1992).

32. Vivian Walsh, "Smith after Sen," *Review of Political Economy*, 12, no. 1 (2000), p. 9.

33. Here Walsh is quoting from my "Objectivity and the Science-Ethics Distinction," p. 148.

34. On this claim, see my "Pragmatism and Moral Objectivity," pp. 170–171.

35. Michele Moody-Adams, *Fieldwork in Familiar Places: Morality, Culture and Philosophy* (Cambridge, Mass.: Harvard University Press, 1997).

36. Williams, *Descartes*, pp. 299–303.

FACT AND VALUE IN THE WORLD OF AMARTYA SEN

1. Amartya Sen, *Development as Freedom* (New York: Anchor Books, 2000), p. 272.

2. A list of Walsh's books and papers on the relations between ethics, economics, and philosophy may be found in the bibliography to his article "Smith after Sen," *Review of Political Economy*, 12, no. 1 (Jan. 2000), p. 25.

3. In "Smith after Sen."

4. Ibid., p. 6.

5. V. C. Walsh, "Normative and Positive Classical Economics," in H. D.

Kurtz and N. Salvadori, eds., *The Elgar Companion to Classical Economics*, vol. 2 (Cheltenham: Edward Elgar, 1998), p. 189.

6. *The Works and Correspondence of David Ricardo*, vol. 1, ed. P. Sraffa and M. H. Dobbs (Cambridge: Cambridge University Press, 1951), p. 6.

7. V. C. Walsh, "Rationality in Reproduction Models," *Conference on Sraffa and Modern Economics* (Rome: Centro Studie Documentazione "Piero Sraffa," 1998), p. 4.

8. Amartya Sen, *On Ethics and Economics* (Oxford: Blackwell, 1987), p. 8.

9. Ibid., p. 57.

10. Adam Smith, *An Inquiry into the Nature and Causes of the Wealth of Nations*, ed. R. H. Campbell and A. S. Skinner (Oxford: Oxford University Press, 1976), pp. 26–27.

11. *On Ethics and Economics*, p. 24. Sen discusses the nature of this misrepresentation of Smith in "Adam Smith's Prudence," in S. Lall and F. Stewart, eds., *Theory and Reality in Development* (London: Macmillan, 1986).

12. An excellent bibliography of Sen's writings with illuminating comments can be found in Steven Pressman and Gale Summerfield, "The Economic Contributions of Amartya Sen," *Review of Political Economy*, 12, no. 1 (Jan. 2000), pp. 89–113.

13. Sen, *On Ethics and Economics*, p. 12.

14. For example, Amartya Sen, "Quasi-Transitivity, Rational Choice and Collective Decisions," *Review of Economic Studies*, 36 (1969), pp. 381–393; *Choice, Welfare and Measurement* (Cambridge, Mass.: MIT Press, 1982); and for recent comments, "Internal Consistency of Choice," *Econometrica*, 61 (1993), pp. 495–521; and "Rationality and Social Choice," *American Economic Review*, 85 (1995), pp. 7–24.

15. Sen argued that it *isn't* cogent because "what we regard as consistent in a set of observed choices must depend on the *interpretation* of those choices and on some features *external* to choice as such (e.g. the nature of our preferences, aims, values, motivations)." *On Ethics and Economics*, p. 14.

16. Ibid., p. 16.

17. John Dewey, *The Middle Works*, vol. 5, ed. Jo Ann Boydston (Carbondale: University of Southern Illinois Press, 1978), p. 257.

18. Ibid.

19. Ibid., pp. 257–258.

20. Robert Nozick, *Anarchy, State, and Utopia* (New York: Basic Books,

1974), pp. 42–45. Here is Nozick's description of the experience machine: "Suppose there were an experience machine that would give you any experience you desired. Superduper neuropsychologists could stimulate your brain so that you would think and feel you were writing a great novel, or making a friend, or reading an interesting book. All the time you would be floating in a tank, with electrodes attached to your brain. Should you plug into this machine for life, preprogramming your life's experiences?" (p. 43). (Nozick answers that you shouldn't.)

21. Ibid., p. 275.
22. Lionel Robbins, "Interpersonal Comparisons of Utility," *Economic Journal*, 48, issue 192 (1938), pp. 635–641.
23. On this, see Walsh's *Rationality, Allocation and Reproduction* (New York: Clarendon, 1996), pp. 179–181.
24. Lionel Robbins, *On the Nature and Significance of Economic Science* (London: Macmillan, 1932), p. 132; quoted by Sen, *On Ethics and Economics,* p. 53.
25. Lionel Robbins, *On the Nature and Significance of Economic Science* (London, 1932), p. 134; quoted by Sen, *On Ethics and Economics,* p. 53.
26. My criticism is reprinted as Chapter 5 of the present volume.
27. *Development as Freedom,* 78–91.
28. The main use of the notion of Pareto optimality, in fact, seems to be in demonstrating the efficiency of free markets, via what is known as the Arrow-Debreu theorem. (This states that, given certain preconditions, the utility—or welfare—of an agent cannot be improved by departing from market mechanisms without lowering the utility—or welfare—of somebody else.) While this is certainly an important and interesting result, it can yield substantive policy recommendations only when coupled with a substantive notion of welfare, as Sen makes clear. (For a Senian explanation of its importance, see *Development as Freedom,* p. 117).
29. *Development as Freedom,* pp. 58–63. See also pp. 304–311.
30. Sen, *Inequality Reexamined* (Cambridge, Mass.: Harvard University Press, 1992), pp. 4–5.
31. Ibid., p. 5.
32. Martha Nussbaum, *Women and Human Development: The Capabilities Approach* (Cambridge: Cambridge University Press, 2000).

33. Sen discusses the shortcomings of the income/wealth information base in detail in Chapter 4 of *Development as Freedom*.
34. *Development as Freedom*, pp. 21–22. Sen also points out that the high mortality rates among black people in America are not adequately explained by the levels of violence in the inner city; they also effect older black males and black women who do not experience violence. One would have to examine, among other things, the American health care system to account for these rates.
35. A brief account of the differences between the various versions may be found in Lawrence C. Becker and Charlotte B. Becker, eds., *Encyclopedia of Ethics*, vol. 2 (New York: Garland, 1992), pp. 1262–1264.
36. *Inequality Reexamined*, p. 55.
37. *Development as Freedom*, p. 77.
38. Ibid.
39. See *Inequality Reexamined*, pp. 46–49.
40. That there is a very important class of (ethical) value-judgments that do not praise or blame anyone was one of the central points of Walsh's *Scarcity and Evil* (Englewood Cliffs, N.J.: Prentice-Hall, 1961). (Walsh's term for the class was "appraisals.")
41. Lionel Robbins, *On the Nature and Significance of Economic Science*, p. 134; quoted by Sen, *On Ethics and Economics*, p. 53.
42. Weber's 1919 lecture "Science as a Vocation" is a classic statement of his position on science and values. It is reprinted in Edward Shils and Henry A. Finch, eds., *Max Weber on the Methodology of the Social Sciences* (New York: Free Press, 1969).
43. *On Ethics and Economics*, p. 89.

SEN'S "PRESCRIPTIVIST" BEGINNINGS

1. Amartya Sen, "The Nature and Classes of Prescriptive Judgments," *Philosophical Quarterly*, 17, no. 66 (1967), pp. 46–62.
2. Ibid., p. 46.
3. Hare, *The Language of Morals* (Oxford: Clarendon Press, 1952).
4. Hare, *Freedom and Reason* (Oxford: Clarendon Press, 1963), p. 16.
5. *The Language of Morals*, pp. 168–169; the text also appears is *Freedom and Reason*, p. 79.
6. Sen, "The Nature and Classes of Prescriptive Judgments," p. 46.
7. Ibid.

8. V. C. Walsh's *Scarcity and Evil* (Englewood Cliffs, N.J.: Prentice-Hall, 1961) contains many examples of ethical judgments that do not imply imperatives, contrary to the "prescriptivist" position.

9. A. J. Ayer, *Philosophical Essays* (London: Macmillan, 1954), p. 237, quoted by Sen, "The Nature and Classes of Prescriptive Judgments," p. 52.

10. Sen, "The Nature and Classes of Prescriptive Judgments," p. 46.

11. Ibid., pp. 46–47.

12. Ibid., p. 26. Sen is quoting from Hare's *Freedom and Reason*.

13. Sen, "The Nature and Classes of Prescriptive Judgments," p. 47.

14. Sen attributes this test (ibid.) to Max Black, "The Gap Between 'Is' and 'Should,'" *The Philosophical Review*, 63 (1964), p. 177.

15. Sen, "The Nature and Classes of Prescriptive Judgments," p. 47.

16. Ibid., p. 48.

17. Among many examples of this are Dudley Shapere, "Notes toward a Post-Positivistic Interpretation of Science," and my "Logical Positivism and the Philosophy of Mind," in Peter Achinstein and Stephen Barker, eds., *The Legacy of Logical Positivism* (Baltimore: The Johns Hopkins Press, 1969), pp. 115–162 and 211–228 respectively. The latter essay is collected in my *Philosophical Papers*, vol. 2: *Mind, Language and Reality* (Cambridge: Cambridge University Press, 1975), pp. 441–455. The Achinstein-Barker collection of essays was an important milestone in the reevaluation of logical positivism. See also my "Explanation and Reference" in *Mind, Language and Reality*, pp. 196–214.

18. Lionel Robbins, *On the Nature and Significance of Economic Science* (London: Macmillan, 1932), p. 134; quoted by Sen, "The Nature and Classes of Prescriptive Judgments," p. 53.

19. Sen, "The Nature and Classes of Prescriptive Judgments," p. 48.

20. Ibid., p. 50.

21. The Ayer passage, quoted by Sen ("The Nature and Classes of Prescriptive Judgments," p. 52), runs as follows: "In what way do these reasons support the judgment? Not in a logical sense. Ethical argument is not formal demonstration. And not in a scientific sense either. For then the goodness or badness of the situation, the rightness or wrongness of the action, would have to be something apart from the situation, something independently verifiable, for which the facts adduced as the reasons for the moral judgment were evidence." Ayer, *Philosophical Essays*, pp. 236–237.

22. Sen, "The Nature and Classes of Prescriptive Judgments," p. 52.
23. Ibid.
24. Hans Reichenbach, *The Rise of Scientific Philosophy* (Berkeley: University of California Press, 1951), Chapter 17.
25. See Hilary Putnam and Ruth Anna Putnam, "Dewey's *Logic:* Epistemology as Hypothesis," and "Education for Democracy," in *Words and Life* (Cambridge, Mass.: Harvard University Press, 1994), pp. 198—220 and 221–241, respectively.
26. Lionel Robbins, *On the Nature and Significance of Economic Science*, p. 132; quoted by Sen, "The Nature and Classes of Prescriptive Judgments," p. 53.
27. Sen, "The Nature and Classes of Prescriptive Judgments," p. 53.
28. Ibid., pp. 53–54.
29. Ibid., pp. 56–59.

ON THE RATIONALITY OF PREFERENCES

Published as: "Über die Rationalit et von Präferenzen," *Allgemeine Zeitschrift für Philosophie*, 21, no. 3, (1996), pp. 209–228. Given at a conference on rationality at Santa Clara University, March 4, 1995. I owe thanks to Vivian Walsh, Amartya Sen, and Thomas Scanlon for close reading, helpful criticism, and constructive suggestions. Warm thanks also to Lisa Walsh, who provided much of the bibliography.

1. "Rationality in Decision Theory and in Ethics," in Shlomo Biderman and Ben-Ami Scharfstein, *Rationality in Question* (Leiden: E. J. Brill, 1989), pp. 19–28. An earlier version appeared in *Critica*, 8, no. 54 (Dec. 1986).
2. Unfortunately, I no longer recall the name of the person who made the response that I shall be discussing.
3. As Vivian Walsh and Amartya Sen both pointed out to me, within economic theory, criticism of the axioms of transitivity and completeness have quite a long history. In "The Pure Theory of Consumer's Behavior," collected in his *Analytical Economics* (Cambridge: Cambridge University Press, 1966), Nicholas Georgescu-Roegen showed that neither assumption is necessary for the theory of consumption. Robert J. Aumann, "Utility Theory without the Completeness Axiom," *Econometrica*, 30 (1962), pp. 445–462; and "A Correction," *Econometrica*, 32 (1964), pp. 210–212, showed that utility theory could be developed

without completeness. Marcel K. Richter and other contributors to Chipman, Hirwicz, Richter, and Sonnenschein, eds., *Preferences, Utility and Demand* (New York: Harcourt Brace Jovanovich, 1971), showed how to dispense with completeness and/or transitivity in treatments of choice, preference, and demand. Sonnenschein, in particular, showed that "the properties of consumer behavior that are necessary to prove the existence, optimality, and unbiasedness or competitive equilibrium depend only on the fact that consumers are maximizing. It follows that the transitivity axiom is both an unnecessary and limiting assumption in the theory of consumer's behavior for competitive equilibrium analysis" (pp. 220–221).

Vivian Walsh points out in *Rationality, Allocation and Reproduction,* (New York: Clarendon, 1996), that there can be little doubt that the axioms of completeness and transitivity had gained a great deal of the prestige that they enjoyed outside economic theory from the vital role that they had played *within* economic theory in the proofs of the canonical existence and optimality theorems of Arrow and Debreu. But by the early 1970s this was no longer true. Following on the work already noted appeared, for example, Andreu Mas-Collel, "An Equilibrium Existence Theorem without Complete or Transitive Preferences," *Journal of Mathematical Economics,* 1 (1974), pp. 237–246; W. J. Shafer, "Equilibrium in Economics without Ordered Preferences or Free Disposal," *Journal of Mathematical Economics,* 33 (1976), pp. 135–137; David Gale and Mas-Collel, "An Equilibrium Existence Theorem for a General Model Without Ordered Preferences," *Journal of Mathematical Economics,* 2 (1975), pp. 9–15; and T. Kim and M. K. Richter, "Non-transitive Non-Total Consumer Theory," *Journal of Economic Theory,* 38 (1986), pp. 324–368. Now the axioms of completeness and transitivity were being dispensed with in the very existence proofs that had once made them famous!

In the special field of social choice theory, both the axiomatic method in general and the axioms of completeness and transitivity were at the very center of Kenneth Arrow's foundational work *Social Choice and Individual Values* (New York: Wiley, 1963). In this area, the weakening and modification of these axioms was initially the work of Amartya Sen, "Quasi-Transitivity, Rational Choice and Collective Decisions," *Review of Economic Studies,* 36 (1969), pp. 381–393; *Choice, Welfare and Measurement* (Cambridge, Mass.: MIT Press, 1982); and more recently, "Internal Consistency of Choice," *Econometrica*, 61 (1993), pp. 495–521; and "Rationality and Social Choice," *American Economic Review*, 85 (1995), pp. 7–24. Using his concept of quasi-transitivity (which involves transitivity of strict preference but not of indifference), Sen was able to show how much Arrow's dramatic negative existence result had depended (among other things) upon *full* transitivity, and how restrictive this was. The truly vast literature that has grown out of Sen's critique of the various axioms involved in social choice theory is indicated by the references to be found in his work. For instance, *Choice, Welfare, and Measurement*, Introduction and Chapters 6, 7, and 8; and *On Ethics and Economics* (Oxford: Blackwell, 1987); and for recent developments, "The Formulation of Rational Choice," *American Economic Review*, 84 (1994), pp. 385–390, as well as the papers cited above from 1993 and 1995.

During roughly the same time period, there has been an equally noteworthy movement critical of completeness and transitivity in the field of decision theory. Some of the themes are the same (as are some of the theorists involved). But the decision theorists have also had their own issues in mind, and a debate that is peculiarly their own has raged over the respective merits of weakening the ordering axioms (completeness and transitivity) and keeping another assumption called "independence" versus giving up independence and retaining orderings. Among those rejecting completeness are Isaac Levi, *Hard Choices* (Cambridge: Cambridge University Press, 1986); Teddy Seidenfeld, "Decision Theory without 'Independence' or without 'Ordering': What is the Difference?" *Economics and Philosophy*, 4 (1988), pp. 267–290; and Paul Anand, "Are the Preference Axioms Really Rational?" *Theory and Decision*, 23 (1993), pp. 189–214.

4. John Von Neumann and Oskar Morgenstern, *Theory of Games and Economic Behavior*, 2nd ed. (Princeton: Princeton University Press, 1947).

5. As noted in n. 3, there are problems with this.

6. For a defense of the idea that goods can be incomparable in the preference ordering of a rational agent along different lines from the present paper, see Isaac Levi, *Hard Choices*.

7. The formula is read: "For every x and for every y, xRy or yRx."

8. "~" is the symbol for negation.

9. See Isaac Levi, *Hard Choices*, on this. See also Vivian Walsh, *Rationality, Allocation and Reproduction*.

10. The smell of fish has been located and analyzed in economic theory, decision theory, and philosophy. For the decision theory literature, see Paul Anand "Are the Preference Axioms Really Rational?" (cf. n. 3); and for a philosophical discussion see Chapter 13 of Joseph Raz's *The Morality of Freedom* (Oxford: Clarendon Press, 1986).

11. The formula is read, "for every x, every y and every z, if both xRy and yRz, then xRz."

12. The formula is read: "for every x, every y and every z, if not-xRy and not-yRz, then not-xRz."

13. Paul Anand is very good on decision theorists who make this sort of move (cf. note 3).

14. "Rationality in Decision Theory and in Ethics," p. 22.

15. Vivian Walsh in *Rationality, Allocation and Reproduction* argues powerfully that this "neutrality" is entirely fictitious.

16. In fact, the idea of construing preference functions as descriptions of real psychological conditions that people are in runs into serious problems with the actual psychological data, as Tamara Horowitz shows in her forthcoming (posthumous, alas) *Decision Theory Naturalized*.

17. See Hilary Putnam, "The Place of Facts in a World of Values," collected in my *Realism with a Human Face* (Cambridge, Mass.: Harvard University Press, 1990).

18. Isaac Levi and Adam Morton, *Disasters and Dilemmas* (Oxford: Clarendon Press, 1991), is very relevant here and takes the position I am defending: that such cases are *not* cases of irrationality.

19. Levi and Morton, ibid., are very good on different *levels* of moral conflict and their possible resolution.

20. T. M. Scanlon, while agreeing with the thrust of my argument has objected to the phrase "not available to the agent prior to the existential choice itself," writing, "I am inclined to resist this phrase. I would be tempted to say of Theresa, as I understand her, that prior to her 'existential choice' she sees the force of reasons for each kind of the two kinds of life and finds them equally balanced in the sense that she thinks that both lives are valuable and that there is good reason for following either path. When she then decides to follow one path, she is not acting from some new reason or reasons but from the very same reasons that she already saw to favor that life. The fact that the two lives are 'incommensurable' in the sense that there are good reasons for following each and no way to compare their value does not mean

that she cannot follow one of these lives simply for the reasons that support *it.*" I think Scanlon is right about *certain* cases—the case of the physician choosing between a wealthy practice and joining Médecins sans Frontières might be of the kind that Scanlon describes—but our original ("Pascalian") case was not of this kind, because accepting the reasons for the religious life as one's reasons entails rejecting the reasons for the sensual life as just plain wrong, and vice versa. Even the doctor's decision could be of this more "existential" kind, if one of the reasons for joining Médecins sans Frontières is that it would be simply selfish (for the person in question) to choose the bourgeois life. In such cases, there is no place prior to the decision from which one can say that the reasons for each are "good."

21. Bernard Williams, "Internal and External Reasons," *Moral Luck* (Cambridge: Cambridge University Press, 1981).

22. Ibid., p. 111.

23. Williams stresses that something can be in one's motivational set without actually being a *means* to some end one acknowledges as one's own; it may, for example, be a way of *better specifying* the content of one of one's acknowledged ends, or it may be a value one did not have the self-consciousness to formulate. But when the "better specification" is one that one is in no way determined to arrive at apart from "nameless environmental factors," the Challenger will ask whether by allowing the former possibility, Williams is not, in fact, allowing certain external reasons to be treated as if they were in some subtle way really "internal."

24. P. F. Strawson, "Ethical Intuitionism," collected in W. Sellars and J. Hospers, eds., *Readings in Ethical Theory* (New York: Appleton-Century-Crofts, 1952).

25. In this connection, Isaac Levi borrows the concept of a second sense of moral struggle—not to *do* what is right but to *find out* what is right—from Dewey and Tufts' *Ethics,* collected in volume 5 of John Dewey, *The Middle Works,* ed. Jo Ann Boydston (Carbondale, Ill.: University of Southern Illinois Press, 1978).

26. If one thinks of how we use expressions like "a good person," "things one ought not to do," and so on, it is not hard to see that these too have some element of "thickness," that is to say descriptive content.

27. Williams, *Moral Luck,* p. 111.

28. See my *Pragmatism* (Oxford: Blackwell, 1995), Chapter 2, for a discussion of Rorty's position.

29. Thus, Williams writes, "one who makes a great deal out of putting the criticism in the form of an external reasons statement seems concerned to say that what is particularly wrong with the person is that he is *irrational*," *Moral Luck*, p. 110. Why should the point of the criticism not be that what is particularly wrong with the person is that, although he subscribes to the virtue of unselfishness, or claims to, he is *selfish?* Or that, although he subscribes to the virtue of kindness, or claims to, he is displaying *cruelty?*

30. Another reason this sort of case is hard to discuss in Williams's framework is the vagueness that he (intentionally) introduces into the notion of one's "motivation set." See n. 23.

31. For a discussion of this sort of oscillation between absurdities see Hilary Putnam, "The Dewey Lectures, 1994: Sense, Nonsense and the Senses—An Inquiry into the Powers of the Human Mind," *Journal of Philosophy*, 91, no. 2 (Sept. 1994), collected as Part I of *The Threefold Cord: Mind, Body and World* (New York: Columbia University Press, 1999); and John McDowell, *Mind and World* (Cambridge, Mass.: Harvard University Press, 1994).

32. Ibid., p. 81. For a brief account of Dewey's view, see Chapter Six in the present volume.

33. Cf. Wittgenstein, *Philosophical Investigations*, §218–§221.

34. For a discussion of the *ethical* uses of the notion of intelligence by John Dewey, see "Pragmatism and Moral Objectivity," collected in Hilary Putnam, *Words and Life* (Cambridge, Mass.: Harvard University Press, 1994).

ARE VALUES MADE OR DISCOVERED?

This essay is a revised version of Hilary Putnam, "Are Moral and Legal Values Made or Discovered?" *Legal Theory*, 1, no. 1 (1995), pp. 5–19. It was originally presented at the Association of American Law Schools Jurisprudence section panel, "On Truth and Justification in the Law," in Orlando, Florida, on January 7, 1994 (Brian Leiter and Jules Coleman were the commentators).

1. See Anat Biletski, *Talking Wolves: Thomas Hobbes on the Language of Politics and the Politics of Language* (Dordrecht: Kluwer, 1997).

2. For a discussion of this aspect of Dewey's thought, see Hilary Putnam and Ruth Anna Putnam, "Dewey's Logic: Epistemology as Hypothe-

sis," collected in Hilary Putnam, *Words and Life* (Cambridge, Mass.: Harvard University Press, 1994).

3. The idea that the axioms of rational preference theory are a priori has been defended—or rather, simply assumed—by Donald Davidson in his well-known papers on the philosophy of mind. See, for example, the papers in Davidson's *Inquiries into Truth and Interpretation* (Oxford: Oxford University Press, 1984). I criticize one of those axioms in Chapter 5.

4. See, in particular, Rorty's *Consequences of Pragmatism* (Minneapolis: University of Minnesota Press, 1982) and the discussions of pragmatism in his *Objectivity, Relativism and Truth: Philosophical Papers, Volume I* (Cambridge: Cambridge University Press, 1991).

5. R. W. Sleeper, *The Necessity of Pragmatism* (New Haven: Yale University Press, 1986), p. 141. Let me say that I disagree with Sleeper's attribution of "the method of tenacity" to William James in the quoted paragraph.

6. For example, in *Philosophy and the Mirror of Nature* (Princeton: Princeton University Press, 1979); in "Solidarity or Objectivity?"; in "Pragmatism, Davidson and Truth" (the latter two are reprinted in *Objectivity, Relativism and Truth*); and in "Putnam and the Relativist Menace," *Journal of Philosophy*, vol. 10 (September 1993), pp. 443–461.

7. Cf. "Solidarity or Objectivity."

8. I discuss it at more length in "The Question of Realism," in *Words and Life* (Cambridge, Mass.: Harvard University Press, 1994), pp. 295–312.

9. This idea, of course, is one that was eloquently defended by Max Weber. See, for example, his "Science as a Vocation," in Edward Shils and Henry A. Finch, eds., *Max Weber on the Methodology of the Social Sciences* (New York: Free Press, 1969).

10. On this, see John McDowell, *Mind and World* (Cambridge, Mass.: Harvard University Press, 1994).

11. For a discussion of this psychology and its survival in both linguistic philosophy and existentialism, see Iris Murdoch, *The Sovereignty of Good* (New York: Schocken Books, 1971). John Dewey was a sharp critic of faculty psychology as well, and much earlier. For example, "the most complex landscape which we can have before our eyes, is, psychologically speaking, not a simple ultimate fact, nor an impression stamped upon us from without, but is built up from color and muscular sensations, with, perhaps, unlocalized feelings of extension,

by means of the psychical laws of interest, attention, and interpretation. It is, in short, a complex judgment involving within itself emotional, volitional, and intellectual elements." From "The New Psychology," in John Dewey, *The Early Works,* vol. 1 (Carbondale: Southern Illinois University Press, 1969), pp. 54–55. And again "The simple fact is that there is no is faculty of observation, or memory, or reasoning any more than there is an original faculty of blacksmithing, carpentering, or steam engineering. These faculties simply mean that particular impulses and habits have been co-ordinated and framed with reference to accomplishing certain definite kinds of work. Precisely the same thing holds of the so-called mental faculties. They are not powers in themselves, but are such only with reference to the ends to which they are put, the services which they have to perform. Hence they cannot be located nor discussed as powers on a theoretical, but only on a practical basis." Ibid., pp. 60–61.

12. The fullest statement of Dewey's account is his *Logic: The Theory of Inquiry* (New York: Henry Holt, 1938). A terse statement is his *The Theory of Valuation* in *The Encyclopedia of Unified Science,* vol. 2, no. 4 (Chicago: University of Chicago Press, 1939). See also the article by H. Putnam and R. A. Putnam cited in n. 2.

13. John Dewey, *Experience and Nature* (LaSalle, Ind.: Open Court, 1926), pp. 407–408.

14. In addition to the paper cited in n. 9, see Hilary Putnam, "A Reconsideration of Deweyan Democracy," and "Afterword," in *Southern California Law Review,* 63 (1990), pp. 1671–1697; and H. Putnam and R. A. Putnam, "Education for Democracy," in *Words and Life.*

15. See Putnam, "Pragmatism and Moral Objectivity," in *Words and Life.*

16. "The Fixation of Belief" is reprinted in *The Collected Papers of Charles Sanders Peirce,* vol. 5: *Pragmatism and Pragmaticism,* eds. Charles Hartshorne and Paul Weiss (Cambridge, Mass.: Harvard University Press, 1965).

17. Variants of this position (often accompanied by incompatible positions and claims) are found in the writings of John Mackie, Gilbert Harman, Bernard Williams, David Wiggins, Simon Blackburn, and Alan Gibbard.

18. I discuss it at length in my *Renewing Philosophy* (Cambridge, Mass.: Harvard University Press, 1990). There are close connections between the irreducibility of normative notions (to physicalist ones) and the ir-

reducibility of semantical notions; indeed, I argue in that work that semantical notions are closely linked to normative ones.

19. This is the view that I defended in *Reason, Truth and History* (Cambridge: Cambridge University Press, 1981). In my Dewey Lectures, published as Part I of *The Threefold Cord: Mind, Body, and World* (New York: Columbia University Press, 1999), I reconsidered and in part retracted that view.

20. This is argued in the first chapter of *Reason, Truth, and History*. For a further discussion, see the paper by Crispin Wright in *Reading Putnam* (Oxford: Basil Blackwell, 1994) and my reply.

21. "Rampant Platonism" was taken from John McDowell's *Mind and World*.

22. This example figures in Iris Murdoch's *The Sovereignty of Good* (New York, Schocken, 1970).

23. On this aspect of pragmatism, see my *Pragmatism: An Open Question* (Oxford: Basil Blackwell, 1994).

24. In "Other Minds," collected in Austin's *Philosophical Papers* (Oxford: Clarendon Press, 1961) p. 84. Most of the points I have attributed to "American pragmatism" in this chapter are also made by Austin—who, like Murdoch, appears not to have read the pragmatists.

VALUES AND NORMS

This is a slightly revised version of a lecture delivered at Johann Wolfgang Goethe Universität in Frankfurt on July 9, 1999, at a conference to honor Jürgen Habermas's seventieth birthday. The lecture has been published (in German translation by Karin Wördemann) as "Werte und Normen" in Lutz Wingert and Klaus Günther, eds., *Die Öffentlichkeit der Vernunft und die Vernunft der Öffentlichkeit: Festschrift für Jürgen Habermas* (Frankfurt am Main: Suhrkamp, 2001), pp. 280–313.

1. "Norms inform decisions as to what one ought to do, values inform decisions as to what conduct is most desirable. Recognized norms impose equal and exceptionless obligations on their addressees, while values express the preferability of goods that are striven for by particular groups. Whereas norms are observed in the sense of the fulfillment of generalized behavioral expectations values or goods can be realized or acquired by purposive action. Furthermore, norms raise a binary validity claim in virtue of which they are said to be either valid

or invalid: to ought statements, as to assertoric statements, we can respond only with 'yes' or 'no'—or refrain from judgment. Values, by contrast, fix relations of preference that signify that certain goods are more attractive than others: hence we can assent to evaluative statements to a greater or lesser degree. The obligatory force of norms has the absolute meaning of an unconditional and universal duty: what one ought to do is equally good for all (that is, for all addressees). The attractiveness of values depends on evaluation and a transitive ordering of goods that has become established in particular cultures or has been adopted by particular groups: important evaluative decisions or higher-order preferences express what is good for us (or for me) all things considered." Habermas, "Reconciliation through the Public Use of Reason: Remarks on John Rawls Political Liberalism," *Journal of Philosophy*, 92, no. 3 (March 1995), pp. 114–115.

2. There is an obvious relation between this and Rawls's analysis of the categorical imperative as a test for maxims, not a means of originating maxims, in *Lectures on the History of Moral Philosophy* (Cambridge, Mass.: Harvard University Press, 2000), pp. 143–325.

3. This example figures centrally in Chapter 1 of Iris Murdoch's *The Sovereignty of Good* (New York: Schocken, 1970), pp. 17–27.

4. Michelle Moody-Adams, *Fieldwork in Familiar Places: Morality, Culture and Philosophy* (Cambridge, Mass.: Harvard University Press, 1997), p. 176.

5. See Hilary Putnam, "A Reconsideration of Deweyan Democracy," *The Southern California Law Review*, 63 (1990), pp. 1671–1698; in addition, see my Preface to *Pursuits of Reason: Essays in Honor of Stanley Cavell*, ed. T. Cohen, P. Guyer, and H. Putnam (Lubbock: Texas Tech Press, 1993), pp. vii–xii; and my "Ein Deutscher Dewey," in *Neue Züricher Zeitung*, 12 (June 13, 1999), p. 77.

6. Christine Korsgaard, with G. A. Cohen, Raymond Geuss, Thomas Nagel, and Bernard Williams, *The Sources of Normativity* (Cambridge: Cambridge University Press, 1996).

7. "Motivation, Metaphysics, and the Value of the Self: A Reply to Ginsborg, Guyer, and Schneewind," *Ethics* 109 (October 1998), pp. 49–66.

8. Iris Murdoch, *Sartre, Romantic Rationalist* (New Haven: Yale University Press, 1953).

9. John Dewey attacked this same picture of the mind back in the 1880s. For example, "the most complex landscape which we can have before

our eyes, is, psychologically speaking, not a simple ultimate fact, nor an impression stamped upon us from without, but is built up from color and muscular sensations, with, perhaps, unlocalized feelings of extension, by means of the psychical laws of interest, attention, and interpretation. It is, in short, a complex judgment involving within itself emotional, volitional, and intellectual elements." From "The New Psychology," in John Dewey, *The Early Works,* vol. 1 (Carbondale: Southern Illinois University Press, 1969), pp. 54–55; and again, "The simple fact is that there is no faculty of observation, or memory, or reasoning any more than there is an original faculty of blacksmithing, carpentering, or steam engineering. These faculties simply mean that particular impulses and habits have been co-ordinated and framed with reference to accomplishing certain definite kinds of work. Precisely the same thing holds of the so-called mental faculties. They are not powers in themselves, but are such only with reference to the ends to which they are put, the services which they have to perform. Hence they cannot be located nor discussed as powers on a theoretical, but only on a practical basis." Ibid., pp. 60–61.

10. In "Motivation, Metaphysics, and the Value of the Self," there is a curious argument designed to show that even valuing *getting what one desires* ("self-love") "is not a causal force that is blocked by another causal force, the moral law, and which therefore operates freely as soon as that other force gets out of the way," but that instead, "It is simply a consideration that has a kind of automatic standing with a self-conscious animal prone to self-love." The argument that the "consideration" of self-love must have this automatic standing is as follows: ". . . could a rational being resist the basic tendency to self-love and therefore deny that her inclinations do have standing? Although Kant seems to deny that this could happen. . . . I see no reason for him to do so, so let us suppose you could. What would follow? You won't be pursuing any personal ends of your own, so what maxims will you consider acting on? We encounter the perfect duties, duties to tell the truth and keep promises and so forth, in the ordinary course of action, going about our business, but now you have no business. How about the imperfect duties? Presumably if you don't regard your own inclinations as having standing, you won't regard the inclinations of others as doing so either, and your duty to promote their happiness will disappear. So what are you going to do...? ...The denial of self-love is a

route to normative skepticism and emptiness, not to freedom from the control of inclination; unless human beings place a value upon ourselves, there can be no reasons and values at all" (pp. 56–57). But surely no one ever, say, ate a pastrami sandwich because they decided to make the maxim of acting on those of their desires which are not morally or prudentially wrong into a law *because they didn't see any other way to avoid normative skepticism.* Even as a rational reconstruction, this is unbelievable.

11. See McDowell, *Mind and World* (Cambridge, Mass.: Harvard University Press, 1994), pp. 84–88, as well as his essay "Two Sorts of Naturalism," in *Mind, Value and Reality* (Cambridge, Mass.: Harvard University Press, 1998), pp. 167–198.

12. The phase is Korsgaard's, in "Motivation, Metaphysics, and the Value of the Self," p. 57.

13. *Reason, Truth, and History* (Cambridge: Cambridge University Press, 1981).

14. *Ethics and the Limits of Philosophy* (Cambridge, Mass.: Harvard University Press, 1985).

15. Cf. Williams's notion of "the absolute conception of the world." For detailed references and discussion, see Chapter 5 of *Renewing Philosophy* (Cambridge, Mass.: Harvard University Press, 1992), pp. 80–107. For a recent exchange between Williams and myself, see his "Philosophy as Humanistic Discipline," *Philosophy*, 75 (2000), pp. 477–496; and my "Reply to Bernard Williams' 'Philosophy as a Humanistic Discipline,'" *Philosophy* 76 (2001), pp. 605–614.

16. I confess to being utterly baffled by the way Williams uses the word "true." See my *Renewing Philosophy*, pp. 103–105.

17. See my essay on Williams, "Pragmatism and Relativism: Universal Values and Traditional Ways of Life," in my *Words and Life* (Cambridge, Mass.: Harvard University Press, 1994), pp. 182–197.

18. Jürgen Habermas and I first met in 1980, when I spent a *Sommersemester* lecturing in Frankfurt at the invitation of another old friend Willi Essler.

19. On Bernard Williams's view, questions framed using the "thin" ethical concepts "should" and "ought" *can* be discussed by people who belong to different "social worlds" provided (i) both social worlds contain those thin ethical concepts (and Williams believes that all contemporary social worlds meet this condition), and (ii) "going over" to the

outlook of the other is a real and not merely a "notional" possibility for both participants in the discussion—and certainly Habermasian discourse ethics would instruct us to treat that as a real possibility, in a case like the one envisaged, for the sake of "communicative action."

20. Frank P. Ramsey, Epilogue ("There Is Nothing to Discuss"), in *Foundations of Mathematics and Other Logical Essays* (London: Routledge and Kegan Paul, 1931), p. 289.

21. Why did I not say, "where the truth lies"? I would say that, too; indeed, in the case of ethics (unlike science), the true view cannot differ from the view for which there are the best reasons, provided we recognize (as Cora Diamond has long urged we should), that ethical reasons cannot always be given as linear arguments. See "Anything But Argument," in Diamond, *The Realistic Spirit* (Cambridge, Mass.: MIT Press, 1991), pp. 291–308.

22. Habermas explicitly relied on Apel's *Tranzendentalpragmatik* in the essays "Wahrheitstheorien," and "Was heisst Universal Pragmatik," collected in his *Vorstudien und Erg nzungen zur Theorie des kommunikativen Handelns* (Frankfurt am Main: Suhrkamp, 1984). For details and references to other places where he did this, see my, "Werte und Normen," in Lutz Wingert and Klaus Günther, eds., *Die Öffentlichkeit der Vernunft und die Vernunft der Öffentlichkeit: Festschrift für Jürgen Habermas*, n. 26.

23. Karl-Otto Apel, *Charles S. Peirce: From Pragmatism to Pragmaticism*, translated by John Michael Krois (Frankfurt am Main: Suhrkamp, 1984).

24. This was anticipated by James (see Hilary Putnam and Ruth Anna Putnam, "William James's Ideas," collected in my *Realism with a Human Face* [Cambridge, Mass.: Harvard University Press, 1990], pp. 217–231); but opposed by Peirce himself—e.g., in *Reasoning and the Logic of Things*, ed. Kenneth Laine Ketner with an introduction by K. L. Ketner and H. Putnam (Cambridge, Mass.: Harvard University Press, 1992), pp. 105–122.

25. Habermas believes that the concept of truth does not apply to norms, although the concept of validity does. This distinction plays a central role in Habermas's reply to the lecture on which this chapter is based, which will appear as "Werte und Normen: Kommentar zu Hilary Putnams Kantischen Pragmatismus," along with my reply, "Antwort auf Jürgen Habermas," in Marie-Louise Raters and Marcus Willaschek, eds., *Hilary Putnam und die Tradition des Pragmatismus* (Frankfurt am

Main: Suhrkamp, 2002). In my "Antwort" I argue that Habermas's view ignores properties of the notion of truth emphasized by the great twentieth-century logicians, particularly Frege and Tarski.

26. See my third Dewey Lecture, "The Face of Cognition," in Putnam, *The Threefold Cord: Mind, Body, and World* (New York: Columbia University Press, 1999), pp. 43–70, as well as my essay "Pragmatism" in *Proceedings of the Aristotelian Society*, 95, part III (1995), pp. 291–306.

27. Among these reasons are destruction of information as a result of normal entropy-increase and the phenomenon called "chaos," as well as fundamental limits to the speed of transmission of information due to relativity theory and to the survival of information due to quantum mechanical phenomena. The last include black holes. A clear popular explanation by Stephen Hawking can be found on the Web at the following address: http://www.hawking.org.uk/text/public/dice.html.

28. I explain my reasons for giving up antirealism with respect to truth in, among other places, my Dewey Lectures, reprinted as Part I of *The Threefold Cord: Mind, Body and World;* "Pragmatism" (cited in n. 26); and "Pragmatism and Realism," *Cardozo Law Review*, 18, no. 1 (September 1996), pp. 153–170, collected in Morris Dickstein, ed., *The Revival of Pragmatism* (Durham: Duke University Press, 1998), pp. 37–53.

29. Apel asserts "dass schon die . . . in jeder Problemerörtung vorausgesetzte rationale Argumentation die Geltung universaler ethischer Normen voraussetzt" ("Das Apriori der Kommunikationsgemeinschaft und die Grundlage der Ethik" in Apel, *Transformation der Philosophie*, vol. 2 (Frankfurt am Main: Suhrkamp, 1976), p. 397. Cf. "Etwas, das ich nicht, ohne einen aktuellen Selbstwiderspruch zu begehen, bestreiten kann, und zugleich ohne formallogische *petitio principii* deduktiv begründen kann, gehört zu jenen transzententalpragmatischen Voraussetzungen der Argumentation, die man immer schon anerkannt haben muss, wenn das Sprachspiel der Argumentation seinen Sinn behalten soll." ("Das Pro-Sprachpragmatik," in B. Kanitschneider, ed., *Sprache und Erkenntnis* (Innsbruck: Institut für Sprachwissenschaft der Universität Innsbruck, 1976), p. 22ff.

30. Cf. the last section ("Was Dewey Trying to Derive an Ethics from the Logic of Science") of "Pragmatism and Moral Objectivity" in my *Words and Life*, pp. 174–177.

31. *The Theory of Communicative Action*, 2 vols., trans. Thomas McCarthy (Boston: Beacon Press, 1984): "Reaching understanding [*Verständigung*]

is considered to be a process of reaching agreement [*Einigung*] among speaking and acting subjects. Naturally, a group of persons can feel as one in a mood which is so diffuse that it is difficult to identify the propositional content or the intentional object to which it is directed. Such a collective like-mindedness [*Gleichgestimmtheit*] does not satisfy the conditions for the type of agreement [*Einverständnis*] at which attempts at reaching understanding terminate when they are successful. A communicatively achieved agreement, or one that is mutually presupposed in communicative action, is propositionally differentiated" (vol. 1, pp. 286–287). And: "If, following Durkheim, we affirm a trend toward the linguistification of the sacred that can be seen in the rationalization of worldviews, in the universalization of law and morality, and in progressive individuation, we have to suppose that the concept of ego-identity will increasingly fit the self-understanding accompanying everyday communicative practice. In this case, we face the serious question of whether, with a new stage of identity formation, the conditions and criteria of identity do not also have to change. Normally, with the answer 'I' a speaker indicates only that he can be identified generically as a speaking and acting subject and numerically by a few significant data that throw light on his background. However, when he satisfies the level of requirement of ego-identity by means of predicative self-identification, he indicates by the answer 'I' (in appropriate contexts) that he can be identified generically as an *autonomously* acting subject and numerically by such data as throw light on the continuity of a life history he has responsibly taken upon himself" (vol. 2, p. 106).

32. Apel, proceeding via a transcendental argument from Peirce's theory of truth as he does, is not forced to face this problem. But once we refuse to identify truth with the consensus that results from (ideal) discussion (and, Peirce would add, *experiment*), the demand for a reason to suppose that truth and consensus coincide in any special case, such as that of ethics, cannot be avoided.

33. *The Sovereignty of Good*, p. 28–37.

34. See n. 10 of this chapter.

35. Note the oxymoronic character of the claim that *we* have no knowledge of the existence of other people! In "Why Reason Can't Be Naturalized" (in my *Philosophical Papers*, vol. 3: *Realism and Reason* [Cambridge: Cambridge University Press, 1983], p. 236) I argued that

Carnap committed exactly this oxymoron in *Der logische Aufbau der Welt*.

36. Here I follow Levinas, as I understand him. See my "Levinas and Judaism," in Robert Bernasconi and Simon Crichley, eds., *The Cambridge Companion to Levinas* (Cambridge: Cambridge University Press, forthcoming).

37. In Chapter 2, the section titled "Epistemic Values Are Values Too."

38. This is why Quine and Bernard Williams regard such talk as without any serious objective content. For Williams's endorsement of Quine's view, see Williams's *Descartes: The Project of Pure Enquiry* (Harmondsworth: Penguin, 1978), pp. 300–303.

39. See *The Many Faces of Realism* (LaSalle, Ill.: Open Court, 1987) pp. 86–90; and *Renewing Philosophy*, pp. 35–55.

40. Ibid., pp. 60–66.

41. See our "Dewey's Logic: Epistemology as Hypothesis," in *Words and Life*, pp. 198–220.

THE PHILOSOPHERS OF SCIENCE'S EVASION OF VALUES

This essay derives from a lecture titled "Philosophy Seen," delivered to the American Philosophical Society for the Advancement of Useful Knowledge in November 1999.

1. In a letter to James dated November 21, 1904, that will be published in a forthcoming volume of *The Correspondence of William James* (Charlottesville, Va.: University of Virginia Press), Dewey wrote "one of the many advantages of the pragmatic approach is that it identifies this ethical problem ['the relation between personal freedom and the stable order'] with the general problem of the relations of the objective and the subjective in experience, instead of leaving the ethical in a small corner by itself."

2. See "Philosophy and the Sciences: A Classification," in Justus Buchler, ed., *The Philosophical Writings of Peirce* (New York: Dover, 1955), pp. 60–73.

3. *The American Evasion of Philosophy* (Madison: University of Wisconsin Press, 1989).

4. But see my distinction between metaphysical and nonmetaphysical uses of "objective" in "Pragmatism and Nonscientific Knowledge," in

NOTES TO PAGES 138–141 | 179

James Conant and Uszula Zeglen (eds.), *Hilary Putnam: Pragmatism and Realism* (London: Routledge, 2002), pp. 14–24.

5. "Two Dogmas of Empiricism," in Quine's *From a Logical Point of View* (Cambridge, Mass.: Harvard University Press, 1953), p. 41.

6. Ibid., p. 46.

7. In Paul Arthur Schilpp, ed., *The Philosophy of Rudolf Carnap* (LaSalle, Ill.: Open Court, 1963), pp. 385–406.

8. The paragraph I quoted ran as follows: "To borrow and adapt Quine's vivid image, if a theory may be black with fact and white with convention, it might well (as far as logical empiricism could tell) be red with values. Since for them confirmation *or* falsification had to be a property of a theory *as a whole*, they had no way of unraveling this whole cloth." Vivian Walsh, "Philosophy and Economics," in *The New Palgrave: A Dictionary of Economics*, vol. 3, ed. J. Eatwell, M. Milgate, and P. Newman (London: Macmillan, 1987), pp. 861–869.

9. Morton White, *Towards Reunion in Philosophy* (Cambridge, Mass.: Harvard University Press, 1956).

10. I have paraphrased a sentence from Quine's *From a Logical Point of View*, p. 44.

11. See, for example, the papers collected in Quine's *Theories and Things* (Cambridge, Mass.: Harvard University Press, 1981).

12 In "Empirical Content," collected in his *Theories and Things*, Quine's notion of "same theory" is as follows: two "theory formulations" are formulations of one and the same theory if (1) they are empirically equivalent (imply the same observational conditionals), and (2) each can be reconciled with the other by reinterpreting its predicates (pp. 24–30).

13. "Epistemology Naturalized," in W. V. Quine, *Ontological Relativity and Other Essays* (New York: Columbia University Press, 1969), p. 75.

14. "Reichenbach and the Limits of Vindication," in my *Words and Life* (Cambridge, Mass.: Harvard University Press, 1994), pp. 131–150.

15. Ernest Nagel, *Principles of the Theory of Probability* (Chicago: University of Chicago Press, 1939).

16. On which, see my "Reichenbach's Metaphysical Picture," in *Words and Life*, pp. 99–114.

17. This is shown in "Reichenbach and the Limits of Vindication."

18. Hans Reichenbach, "Are Phenomenal Reports Absolutely Certain,"

Philosophical Review, 61, no. 2 (April 1952), pp. 147–159. For a discussion, see my "Reichenbach and the Myth of the Given," in *Words and Life*, pp. 115–130.

19. In fact, in his response to my "'Degree of Confirmation' and Inductive Logic," in *The Philosophy of Rudolf Carnap* (La Salle, Ill.: Open Court, 1963), Carnap backs away significantly from the hopes for an algorithm that would enable us to reproduce the judgments of an ideal inductive judge he expressed in *Logical Foundations of Probability* (Chicago: University of Chicago Press, 1950), his only book-length treatment of inductive logic. For a proof that Carnap's project could not do that, see my "'Degree of Confirmation' and Inductive Logic."

20. Although the view is much older, it was influentially put forward by Quine in his celebrated "Two Dogmas of Empiricism," collected in Quine's *From a Logical Point of View*, pp. 20–46.

21. The refutation of Whitehead's theory was the work of C. M. Will, "Relativistic Gravity in the Solar System, II: Anisotrophy in the Newtonian Gravitational Constant," *Astrophysics Journal*, 169 (1971), pp. 409–412.

22. It is also worth pointing out that Popper repeatedly claims that the famous eclipse experiment was an *experimentum crucis*, and thus illustrates the superior "falsifiability" of Einstein's general relativity. In fact, the experiment produced four sets of results; depending on which of the (poor quality) photographs one trusted, one got Einsteinian deviation, Newtonian deviation, and even double Einsteinian deviation! Really solid experimental confirmation of general relativity came only in the 1960s. For an account of this confirmation, see Charles W. Misner, Kip S. Thorne, and John Archibald Wheeler, *Gravitation* (San Francisco: Freeman, 1973), Part IX. That general relativity was accepted before there were decisive experiments in its favor of course contradicts completely the whole Popperian account, which can be characterized as mythological.

23. For a devastating critique of this idea, and of the way it has infected cultural anthropology since the days of Herder, see Michele Moody's *Fieldwork in Familiar Places: Morality, Culture and Philosophy* (Cambridge, Mass.: Harvard University Press, 1997).

24. See Alvin Goldman, *Epistemology and Cognition* (Cambridge, Mass.: Harvard University Press, 1986). I thank Jamie Tappenden for suggesting I discuss this alternative.

25. This objection to reliabilism was suggested to me by Ernest Nagel's objection to Reichenbach's views on the justification of theories (views that were, themselves, of a "reliabilist" character). See Ernest Nagel, "Probability and the Theory of Knowledge," *Philosophy of Science*, 6 (1939), pp. 212–253; and *Principles of The Theory of Probability, International Encyclopedia of Unified Science*, vol. 1, no. 6, (Chicago: University of Chicago Press, 1939).

26. It might be claimed that judgments of reasonableness are carried out according to an unconscious algorithm built into our brains. This presupposes the success of a computationalist account of scientific rationality. For a criticism of this presupposition, see my *Representation and Reality* (Cambridge, Mass.: MIT Press, 1988); and the article "Putnam, Hilary" in Samuel Guttenplan, ed., *A Companion to the Philosophy of Mind* (Oxford: Blackwell, 1994), pp. 507–513; and "Reflexive Reflections," *Erkenntnis*, 22 (1985), pp. 143–153, collected in *Realism with a Human Face* (Cambridge, Mass.: Harvard University Press, 1990). It is also not clear why such an account of how our brains work should yield a factorization of the various arguments we accept into "methods" of the kind required by reliabilist epistemology.

INDEX

Absoluteness, 41, 42, 44, 45, 119, 120
Aesthetics, 19, 135
Analytic, 17, 18, 21, 29–30, 61
Analytic judgment, 10
Analytic-synthetic distinction, 7–8, 9–13, 14, 18, 29, 68
Analytic truth, 8, 12, 13, 16
Anderson, Elizabeth, 36–37, 43, 71
Antirealism, 123–124
Antiskepticism, 110
Apel, Karl Otto, 122, 123–124, 125, 126, 127, 129, 130, 176n29, 177n32
A priori, 8, 11, 17
Aristotle, 43, 134
Arrow, Kenneth, 163n3
Assertibility, warranted, 103, 104, 106–109, 110, 144. See also Justification

Aumann, Robert J., 163n3
Austin, John, 110, 171n24
Authoritarianism, 114
Autonomy, 83–86
Ayer, A. J., 69, 74, 76, 77

Bentham, Jeremy, 51
Berkeley, George, 21, 40
Bravery, 39–40

Campbell, Norman, 23
Capability, 49, 56–60, 62–63, 73
Capacity, for valuable functions, 62–63
Carnap, Rudolf: and ethics, 17–18, 19, 20, 24–25, 151n26; The Unity of Science, 18, 19; Der logische Aufbau der Welt, 22; and facts, 22–23, 30; and verifiability, 22–23, 152n33;

Carnap, Rudolf (*continued*)
"Foundations of Logic and Mathematics," 23; and language, 24–25, 26, 153n39, 154nn42,43; and science, 25, 141, 145, 180n19; and hypothesis-selection, 31; and analytic, 149nn11,12; and Ricketts, 153n38
Categorical imperative, 114, 115. *See also* Imperative
Causation, 21, 22
Choice, consistency of, 49, 50
Churchland, Paul, 154n45
Churchman, C. West, 136
Clarke, Samuel, 152n30
Commodity, 83
Commodity bundle, 80
Communicative action, 112, 113–115, 121, 122, 125. *See also* Discourse
Concept: and Carnap, 24; thick ethical, 35–36, 39, 62, 72, 91, 118, 119, 120–121, 122, 128, 129–130, 132; factorability of, 36, 38–39, 62, 69, 118, 119; thin ethical, 91. *See also* Idea
Contextualism, 132
Convention, 8, 10, 11, 30, 138
Crime, 20, 35, 39
Cruelty, 34, 38, 39, 40
Culture, 44, 45, 60, 99, 120, 143

Davidson, Donald, 25, 85, 169n3
Decision theory, 81, 82. *See also* Preference
Democracy, 104–105, 110, 114
Deprivation, 58–59
Descartes, René, 107, 108
Description: and Carnap, 24–25, 26; and epistemic values, 32–33; and language, 33, 34, 35; and factorability, 36, 38–39, 62, 118, 119; and thick ethical concepts, 36; and noncognitivism, 38–39; and evaluation, 39–40; and values, 62; and Sen, 69, 73; and Peirce, 124
Desire, satisfaction of, 58–59
Dewey, John: and fact/value distinction, 9, 11, 61, 98; and normative judgments, 30; and fallibilism, 45, 133; and Bentham, 51, 52; and Sen, 77; and objectivity, 94; and values, 97–98, 101–106, 110, 135, 178n1; and discourse ethics, 125; and naturalism, 130; and psychology, 169n11, 172n9
Diamond, Cora, 175n21
Dichotomy vs. distinction, 9, 10, 11, 60–61
Discourse: rational, 17–18, 20–21, 54, 113; scientific vs. ethical, 119; and communicative action, 125. *See also* Language
Discourse ethics, 105, 112, 115, 116–117, 119, 120–123, 125, 126, 128–129, 130, 133–134
Diversity, of ideals, 113
Dualism, 9, 10, 11, 61
Duty, objective, 89–90

Economics, 46–60, 62–64, 73, 74
Edgeworth, Francis Ysidro, 52–53
Einstein, Albert, 144
Emotion, 15, 17, 20, 36, 102
Empiricism: and fact/value distinction, 9, 26–27, 28; and logical positivism, 10, 29; and mathematics, 13; and Carnap, 23, 24; and facts, 40; and values, 102–103; and truth, 124; and Einstein, 144. *See also* Science
Entanglement: of fact and value, 28–45, 72, 74; and evaluation, 62, 63, 64
Epistemic value, 30–34, 132, 143
Epistemology, 44, 102, 139, 144

Error theory, 35, 43
Ethics: and Hume, 15, 16, 17, 18, 19–20, 29; and Carnap, 17–18, 19, 20, 24–25; and reason, 17–18, 44, 74–78; and discourse, 17–18, 105, 112, 115, 116–117, 119, 120–123, 125, 126, 128–129, 133–134; and facts, 19; and logical positivism, 19, 20–21, 22; and pragmatism, 31; and epistemic values, 31–34; and fact/value entanglement, 34–43; and thick concepts, 35–36, 39, 62, 72, 91, 118, 119, 120–121, 122, 128, 129–130, 132; and Hare, 36–37, 68; and Williams, 41, 44; and Mackie, 42–43; and Adams, 44; and metaphysics, 44, 94–95; and Sen, 47–48, 67; and economics, 49–56, 63–64, 74; and Robbins, 54, 63; and Weber, 63; and subjectivity, 74; and preference, 90; and noncognitivism, 90–91; and thin concepts, 91; and warranted assertibility, 103, 104, 106–109, 110; and Habermas, 105, 120–123, 125, 126, 127, 128, 129, 130, 132–133, 174n19; and objectivity, 106; and science, 106; and verification, 108, 124–125; and Kant, 116–117; and Dewey, 125; and naturalism, 130–131; and judgment, 131; and justification, 131; and knowledge, 132; and Peirce, 135. See also Morality; Value; Value judgment
Evaluation. See Value; Value judgment
Experience, 30, 103, 135
Experiment, 12, 105, 110

Fact: and value judgments, 7, 76, 78, 108; and logical positivism, 8, 12, 19, 21, 22, 23–24, 26, 28–29, 34, 40, 61; and Quine, 12, 13, 30; and

Hume, 13, 14, 15, 17, 20, 21, 22, 26, 28, 35, 40; and Kant, 17; and ethics, 19; and values, 19, 27, 28–45, 43, 137, 145; and fact/value distinction, 19–24; and Carnap, 22–23, 30; natural, 39, 40; and empiricism, 40; and Williams, 40–42; and Mackie, 42; and Robbins, 63; and Sen, 68, 69, 78; and Dewey, 97, 98, 104; and theory, 136, 137, 141; and convention, 138; and knowledge, 141, 145
Factorability, of concepts, 36, 38–39, 62, 69, 118, 119
Fact/value distinction, 7, 9, 14–24, 26, 35, 40, 43–45, 98, 102
Fallibilism, 45, 102, 110, 133
Firth, Roderick, 32
Freedom, 59, 60
Free will, 82, 83, 84–85
Frege, Gottlob, 8, 147n1, 148n5
Functionings, 56–57, 60

Georgescu-Roegen, Nicholas, 163n3
Goldman, Alvin, 144
Good, 20, 43, 80, 81, 82

Habermas, Jürgen: and means-ends rationality, 98; and discourse ethics, 105, 120–123, 125, 126, 127, 128, 129, 130, 132–133, 174n19; and values vs. norms, 111–117; and truth, 122, 175n25; The Theory of Communicative Action, 128
Hare, R. M., 35, 36–37, 62, 69, 70–71, 72, 75, 77; The Language of Morals, 67–68
Herman, Barbara, 17, 115
Hobbes, Thomas, 96–97
Hume, David: and facts, 13, 14, 15, 17, 20, 21, 22, 26, 28, 35, 40; and is vs. ought, 14–16, 28, 149n13; Enquiry

Hume, David (*continued*)
  Concerning the Principles of Morals,
    16; and logical positivism, 17, 21,
    29; and ethics, 18, 19–20, 29; and
    morality, 20; and science, 21,
    152n29; and fact/value distinction,
    28, 61; and Mackie, 39; and free
    will, 84; and Stevenson, 150n16
Hypothesis. *See* Theory

Idea, 9, 14, 15, 26. *See also* Concept
Imperative: and Kant, 16–17; and value
    judgments, 67, 68, 69, 70–72; and
    Sen, 70, 75; and Reichenbach, 77;
    and Habermas, 114, 115
Indifference, 81, 82, 83
Induction, 45, 139–140, 141
Is vs. ought, 9, 14–16, 28

James, William, 30, 99, 130, 136, 137
Jevons, William Stanley, 52, 53
Judgment: cognitively meaningful, 10,
    22, 23, 24, 25, 29, 34, 61; and logical
    positivism, 10, 17; and mathematics,
    11; and Kant, 11, 17; and Hume, 17;
    ethical vs. non-ethical, 19; normative,
    30–31; prescriptive vs. evaluative,
    69–70; and Sen, 69–70, 75; compul-
    sive vs. noncompulsive, 70, 75; and
    ethics, 131. *See also* Value judgment
Justification, 32, 33, 125, 131, 137, 143.
    See also Assertibility, warranted

Kant, Immanuel: and analytic-synthetic
    distinction, 8, 11, 18, 147n1; and
    logical positivism, 8; and synthetic,
    8, 11, 13; and judgment, 11; and
    fact/value distinction, 16–17; and
    Dewey, 98; and perception, 102; and
    Habermas, 112, 115, 116; and dis-
    course ethics, 116–117; and Kors-
    gaard, 117, 118; and values, 118,
    119, 129; and human flourishing,
    134; and Peirce, 135
Knowledge, 21, 45, 131–132, 136, 137,
    141, 145
Kohlberg, Lawrence, 36
Korsgaard, Christine, 17, 113, 115,
    117–118, 119, 120

Language: and analytic-synthetic dis-
    tinction, 10; and logical positivism,
    24–27, 29, 34; and description, 33,
    34, 35; and fact/value entangle-
    ment, 34, 62; and science, 34; and
    Williams, 40–41, 91; and objective
    reality, 100; and morality, 109, 119;
    thick ethical, 122, 128. *See also*
    Discourse
Law, 96, 97, 106, 108, 109, 120
Levi, Isaac, 167n25
Lewis, C. I., 141
Lewis, David, 155n46
Life world, 112, 117
Locke, John, 21
Logic, 10, 29, 33
Logical positivism: and facts, 8, 12, 19,
    21, 22, 23–24, 26, 28–29, 34, 40, 61;
    and Kant, 8, 11; and mathematics, 8,
    17, 29; and synthetic, 8, 61; and judg-
    ment, 10; and science, 11, 12, 22, 23,
    24, 29, 34; and analytic, 17, 21, 29, 61;
    and Hume, 17, 29; and values, 18, 19,
    28–29; and ethics, 19, 20–21, 22; and
    rational discourse, 20–21; and lan-
    guage, 24–27, 29, 34; and Mackie, 43;
    and choice, 50; and Robbins, 53, 54;
    and Sen, 69, 74, 77; and meaning, 74;
    and skepticism, 131
Lyotard, Jean-François, 129, 130

Mackie, John, 35, 36, 39, 40, 42–43, 62

Manipulation, 114–115, 125, 127
Marshall, Alfred, 52, 53
Materialism, 131
Mathematics: and logical positivism, 8, 17, 29; and judgment, 11; and Kant, 11; and Quine, 12, 30; and empiricism, 13; and Hume, 21; and objectivity, 33; and metaphysics, 45
McDowell, John, 35, 38–39, 62, 94, 119
Meaning, 38, 74
Metaphysics: and logical positivism, 10, 11; and Hume, 14–15; and Kant, 17; and fact/value distinction, 40; and Williams, 41, 42, 44, 92; and Mackie, 43; and ethics, 44, 94–95; and mathematics, 45; and dichotomy, 61; and science, 94; and antirealism, 124; and Habermas, 133; and Reichenbach, 140
Moody-Adams, Michele, 44, 116
Moore, G. E., 128
Morality: and Kant, 17; and Hume, 20; and pragmatism, 31; and Dewey, 51; and welfare economics, 57; and Hobbes, 96, 97; and realism, 108–109; and Habermas, 112; and Moody-Adams, 116; and language, 119; and perception, 128. See also Ethics; Value; Value judgment
Morgenstern, Oskar, 79, 80
Motivation, 36–37, 49, 50–52, 64, 71, 72, 90, 93
Murdoch, Iris, 35, 38, 62, 118, 128, 171n24; The Sovereignty of Good, 40

Nagel, Ernest, 140, 181n25
Naturalism, 130–131, 133
Newton, Isaac, 152n30
Noncognitivism: and Hume, 20; and thick ethical concepts, 35–36, 38, 39; and relativism, 41; and fact/value

entanglement, 43; and Sen, 67, 69; and ethics, 90–91; and Habermas, 112; and value judgments, 137; and values, 142
Nonsense, 25, 34
Norm, 111–134
Normativity, 30, 31, 34, 35
Nozick, Robert, 51, 52, 64, 159n20
Nussbaum, Martha, 57

Objectivity: and epistemic values, 32, 33; and Mackie, 39; and culture, 45; and Dewey, 45, 99; and agreeableness, 51; and Rorty, 99, 143; and reality, 99–101; and ethics, 106; and value judgments, 108; and Kant, 116; and Habermas, 133; and justification, 137; and pragmatism, 145; and reasonableness, 145
Obligation, 13, 112, 132
Observation, 12, 13, 41, 105, 142. See also Perception; Sense
Observation statement, 140, 141
Observation term, 23, 24–25, 26, 29, 34
Other, as end and means, 112, 115

Pareto optimality, 54, 56
Peirce, Charles Sanders, 30, 31, 32, 41, 99, 102, 123, 124, 125, 135, 140; "The Fixation of Belief," 105
Perception, 102, 109–110, 128. See also Observation; Sense
Physics, 11, 12, 23, 40, 41, 106, 138. See also Science
Picture, 13, 15
Pigou, Arthur Cecil, 53, 55, 60
Pleasure, 51, 52
Popper, Karl, 141, 142, 145, 180n22
Positivism, 55–56, 96, 112, 133. See also Logical positivism

Pragmatism, 30–31, 102, 103, 109, 110, 136, 138, 145
Predicate, 22, 29, 34, 36
Preference, 49, 79–95, 112
Prescription, 38, 39, 62, 69
Prescriptivism, 68, 70–71, 72, 75
Problem, solving of, 45, 97–98, 108–109
Psychology, 26, 117, 118, 128, 129, 139, 145
Putnam, Ruth Anna, 104, 133

Quine, Willard van Orman, 8, 13, 29–30, 137–138, 139, 141–142, 145, 178n38, 179n12; "Two Dogmas of Empiricism," 12; "Carnap and Logical Truth," 138

Rand, Ayn, 114, 115
Rawls, John, 17, 64, 115, 172n2
Realism, 123, 124, 139, 143
Reality, objective, 99–101
Reasonableness, 144, 145
Reason/rationality: and discourse, 17–18, 54, 113; and values, 44; and economics, 49–50; and value judgments, 67, 70, 76; and ethics, 74–78; and preference, 79–95; and Kant, 117, 118, 129; and Apel, 125
Reasons: desire for, 85, 86–88; internal vs. external, 88–92
Reichenbach, Hans, 19, 77, 137, 139–141, 145, 151n26, 181n25
Relativism, 41, 43, 44, 45, 120, 132, 142, 143
Representation, 100–101
Ricardo, David, 47
Richter, Marcel K., 163n3
Ricketts, Thomas, 153n38
Robbins, Lionel, 53–54, 60, 61, 63, 64, 74, 77
Rorty, Richard, 92, 98, 121, 143

Scanlon, T. M., 166n20
Science: and Quine, 8, 12, 30; and logical positivism, 11, 12, 21, 22, 23, 24, 29, 34; and Carnap, 18, 23, 25, 141; and Hume, 21; and value, 30, 31, 135–145; philosophy of, 30–31, 131, 135–145; and pragmatism, 30–31; and language, 34; and fact/value distinction, 40, 102; and Williams, 40, 41, 119; and Walsh, 42; and Weber, 63; and value judgments, 76, 135, 136, 137, 138, 142, 143–144, 145; and metaphysics, 94; and fallibilism, 102; and ethics, 106; and discourse, 119; and Peirce, 124; and truth, 124; and moral perception, 128; and knowledge, 131–132, 136, 137, 141, 145; and epistemic values, 132; and Popper, 141. See also Empiricism
Self-discovery, 89, 90
Self-interest, 48, 49, 50–51, 52
Selfishness, 49–50, 91–92
Self-love, 48, 49
Sen, Amartya, 46–60, 62, 63, 64, 67–78, 159n15, 160n28, 161n34, 163n3; Development as Freedom, 59; Ethics and Economics, 64; "The Nature and Classes of Prescriptive Judgments," 67
Sense, 21, 22, 138. See also Perception
Sense impression, 40
Sentiment. See Emotion
Singer, A. E., Jr., 136, 141
Skepticism, 131–132
Sleeper, Ralph, 98–99
Smith, Adam, 47, 48–49, 50, 60
Socrates, 39–40, 44, 74
Solidarity, 99, 100
Sonnenschein, Hugo F., 163n3
Sovereign, 96, 97

Sraffa, Piero, 47
Stevenson, Charles Leslie, 20, 150n16, 151n26; *Facts and Values*, 19
Subjectivity: and value judgments, 7, 44, 61; and values, 31; and Bentham, 51; and pleasure, 52; and utility, 55; and ethics, 74; and Sen, 74; and justification, 137; and pragmatism, 145
Synthetic, 8, 11, 13, 61
Synthetic judgment, 10

Tautology, 8, 61
Theoretical term, 24, 25, 26, 29, 34
Theory: and fact/value distinction, 26, 30; selection of, 31–32, 138, 139, 140, 141–142; and facts, 136, 137, 141; and knowledge, 141
Truth: analytic, 8, 12, 13, 16; and epistemic values, 32; and warranted assertibility, 106–109; and value judgments, 110; and Williams, 120; and Apel, 122, 123–124, 125; and empiricism, 124; and science, 124
Truth-telling, 113, 114–115

Utilitarianism, 51, 56, 58, 63–64, 78
Utility, 52–53, 54–55, 80

Validity, 33, 122–123
Valuation. See Value; Value judgment
Value: and logical positivism, 8, 19, 28–29; term of, 18, 19, 71; and facts, 19, 27, 28–45, 137, 145; and experience, 30; and science, 30, 31, 135–145; epistemic, 30–34, 132, 143; and subjectivity, 31; and theory selection, 31; ethical, 31–34; and Mackie, 39; and rationality, 44; and choice, 50; and neutrality, 54, 56; and economics, 56, 62–64; and de-

scription, 62; and Weber, 63; basic vs. non-basic, 70; and Hobbes, 96–97; and Dewey, 97–98, 101–106, 110, 135, 178n1; and empiricism, 102–103; and perception, 102–103; and criticism, 103, 104, 109, 110; and Habermas, 112; and Korsgaard, 117–118; and factorability, 118, 119; and Kant, 118, 119, 129; and justification, 137; and knowledge, 141, 145; and noncognitivism, 142. *See also* Ethics
Valued vs. valuable, 103
Value judgment: and facts, 7, 76, 78, 108; and subjectivity, 7, 61; and Kant, 16–17; and Carnap, 24; and Hare, 36–37, 68; and description, 39–40; distinctions in, 60–61; and imperatives, 67, 68, 69, 70–72; and reason, 67, 70, 74, 76; and Sen, 67, 68–70, 72–74, 75, 78; and Ayer, 69; basic vs. non-basic, 75–78; and science, 76, 135, 136, 137, 138, 142, 143–144, 145; compulsive vs. noncompulsive, 77; and warranted assertibility, 103, 104, 106–109, 110; and Dewey, 104; and objectivity, 108; and truth, 110; and Korsgaard, 117; and noncognitivism, 137. *See also* Judgment
Variable, internal vs. external, 84
Verification/verifiability, 22–23, 25, 74, 107–109, 124
Vienna circle, 22. *See also* Logical positivism
Von Neumann, John, 47, 54, 79, 80

Walsh, Vivian, 30, 42, 47, 49, 53, 64, 138, 163n3, 166n15; *Scarcity and Evil*, 57
Weber, Max, 63

Welfare economics, 48, 49, 52, 56, 57, 73. *See also* Economics

Well-being, 58, 62, 63

White, Morton, 30, 137, 138

Wiggins, David, 35

Williams, Bernard: and facts, 40–42; and metaphysics, 44; and reasons, 89; and thick ethical concepts, 91, 119–120, 122–123; and thin ethical concepts, 91, 174n19; and irrationality, 92, 93, 94; and absoluteness, 119, 120; *Ethics and the Limits of Philosophy,* 119; and norms, 121; and motivation, 167n23, 168n30; and selfishness, 168n29; and Quine, 178n38

Wingrave, Owen, 91

Wittgenstein, Ludwig, 87, 126, 127